WORK LIKE A SLAVE, THINK LIKE A MASTER

WORK LIKE A SLAVE, THINK LIKE A MASTER

Are You Working Like a Slave Toward Mastery and Thinking Like a Master Toward your Mission?

Collis Temple III

Foreword by Dale Brown

ISBN: 0997033606
ISBN 13: 9780997033601
Temple Life Publishing: **Baton Rouge, Louisiana**

To my parents for EVERYTHING!

To my wife, Britney, for pushing me to do this.

To my children—Monet, Eden, and Collis IV—for giving me the opportunity to be EVERYTHING for them.

CONTENTS

ACKNOWLEDGMENTS

I would like to thank my wife, Britney, for her continued love and support. Thank you also for your dogged persistence that I get this book done and share my story, and for being the first to believe that my story could make a difference and truly help others. Thank you for always forcing me to look at ways to improve and grow. I thank my children for constantly teaching me the biggest and most important leadership lessons every day and forcing me to be more accountable for everything.

Thank you to my family—my parents, Collis Jr. and Soundra Temple-Johnson, and siblings, Elliott, Garrett, and Colleen. All these lessons have come from experiences that you helped me through, and I would never have wanted it any other way.

Thank you to all the other people who've entrusted me with the opportunity to lead them and those who've enabled me to grow and learn from them as a leader. Thank you to Bill Whittle for teaching me business his way, and for being so consistent. Thank you to Yvette and Eddie Henderson for being the first couple to buy into my vision. Thank you to Tammy Williams for her trustworthiness, honesty, and work ethic as my executive assistant and office manager. I would be remiss if I didn't thank the amazing team of business partners and up-and-coming leaders whom I am blessed to be able to work with every day. You inspire me to be better, stretch further, and be a greater example. You make me look better than I am.

Thank you to so many friends and mentors in business and life; there are so many that there are not enough pages to cover all of them. Thank you to the entire Primerica and African-American Leadership Council (AALC) families for help, guidance, leadership, and so much more. People like Ivan Earle, Mike Evans, John Addison, Glenn Williams, and Rick Williams have made huge differences in my life. Thank you to Art Williams for having a big vision and the courage to correct an injustice.

Most of all I'd like to thank God for giving me the amazing fortune of placing me where he has, with whom he has, to do what he's placed me here to do. I understand why I'm here, and I don't take my mission for granted.

FOREWORD

Work like a Slave, Think like a Master by Collis Temple III should be read by all people because it would put them on the path to peace, love, happiness, and success.

After all the ugly things the Temple family had to endure for several generations, instead of becoming bitter they chose to become better through family, love, unity, discipline, and education. They represent the paramount example that if you want to improve your life it starts with hard work, no excuses, perseverance, spirituality, commitment, and education.

—Dale Brown, Louisiana State University
Head Basketball Coach 1972–1997

INTRODUCTION

This book is a work that I can by no means take sole credit for creating. I say that because it only exists due to knowledge, information, will, hard work, and perseverance that were demonstrated in large part before I was even born. I was simply the willing beneficiary of receiving and, more important, implementing these pearls of wisdom that I hope have a positive impact on whoever decides that it would be worth their time to read these pages.

I've always said that everyone has his or her own story, and many people's stories revolve around the idea of coming up from rags to riches with limited assistance from anyone else. That was not my story. Having lived on this earth for slightly over a third of a century, I have been blessed and aided all along the way to achieve the modest level of success that I have to this point in my life. The genesis of the idea behind writing this book came as a result of my initial success in business. I would be asked by others, when I would take occasional speaking opportunities, to put on paper the ideals that I was raised with that led to my success-driven thought process. The success-driven thought process is not at all abnormal for those who have experienced success in any area during their lives. But my ability to articulate this way of thinking has helped thousands of people feel it was something that they could program or reprogram by themselves in reference to their own thought process. As a result of the numerous conversations about the impact my talks were making, along with being pushed to do it by my amazing wife, I was led to write *Work like a Slave, Think like a Master.*

"No, this is where you're SUPPOSED to be! This is how things have been designed for you." That was the answer that my dad, Collis Temple Jr., gave me in July 2007 as we stood on the balcony of my newly constructed home overlooking the tenth hole of the golf course. It was a home that many might consider to be a dream home, and I had worked hard enough, been coachable enough, and stayed focused for long enough to have done it after less than four years in business. The answer he gave me was the by-product of me looking at him, smiling, and saying, "This is unbelievable, isn't it, Dad?" My parents taught me that things didn't happen by accident, but by design, and that I was the architect who could put what I wanted into existence.

Work like a Slave, Think like a Master is set up to take the reader from the early stages of the mentality-shaping process at a young age through to adulthood, using that same mentality to create and re-create success after success. The book illustrates a way of thinking that has helped me experience success in several unrelated areas of life. It starts with some of the challenges and triumphs that shaped my early thoughts and moves on to my growth and development into manhood and the adaptation of the same success principles in my life as a young adult. I've learned that, many times, successful athletes have an unfortunate inability to transfer the mind-set that has helped them excel in their chosen sport to some other area of their lives. Because of the baseline I was programmed with, I was able to duplicate the successes from other areas throughout my life based on simply transferring those ways of thinking and processing situations that were responsible for success. Notice that I used the word *programmed*, because that is truly what it comes down to. Fortunately, we are in control of programming ourselves and designing our success. This book is my journey to learn and implement these ideas.

I start off with a brief history of my family in the hopes that it will show that although many great people built their mentality from outside of their immediate circle, in my case, there was a linage of success that I was fortuitously able to mentally lean on and build upon and that aided me in that process. Just because you may not have giants to stand on the shoulders of, as I have, doesn't mean you can't experience your own amazing levels of success; it just means you may have to borrow someone else's giants and use their experiences to learn and grow to the level you want to achieve!

I've been told that the title of the book may come across as being offensive, but when I talk about working like a slave and thinking like a master, I'm referring to working like a slave tirelessly toward GREATNESS and MASTERY of whatever you endeavor to achieve, and thinking like a master toward an amazing VISION and FUTURE to ultimately accomplish your MISSION. Be a SLAVE to the daily habits and practices that will lead to your success in whatever you endeavor to succeed at. Be a MASTER of your thoughts with the mentality that the future will be amazingly better and will yield success beyond your wildest imagination, because you are going to WILL it and WORK it into existence!

At the end of each chapter in this book you'll find "WSTM Lessons Learned." WSTM, of course, is an abbreviation of the book's title. The Lessons Learned present primary points that, in addition to whatever you gain from the chapters on your own, should be pulled out, focused on, and hopefully implemented from each chapter. This is a biography, but its purpose is to teach based on experiences, and the "WSTM Lessons Learned" should serve as a great place to start.

This book is designed to serve as a GPS of sorts to lead to success in any area in which a person desires to become successful. The stories in this book should serve as lessons in building a thought process conducive to making SUCCESS a way of life and not a one-time occurrence.

Collis Temple III

Part I

BEFORE COLLEGE

Chapter 1

A SOLID FOUNDATION

If you're succeeding without suffering,
someone else already did.
If you're suffering without succeeding,
someone else will. —Anonymous

"NEW GENERATION OF TEMPLES"-1989, Fourth Grade, Nine Years Old

My hero is my father. I would like to be like him in almost every way. My father is a great man because of the way he was brought up as a child. His mother was a school teacher and his father was a principal at the same school. They both disciplined my father very well and that's why he is in this place now.

This is how it went, my dad went to Kentwood High School. There, he played football and basketball. Soon he got to go to LSU. He became the first Afro-American to play basketball at LSU. He was an All-American. The thing that I like most about this is that he was (more important than basketball), the first Afro-American athlete to graduate from LSU! He played football also! He was drafted to the NFL and the NBA. He chose the NBA and played for three years.

He got married to a beautiful woman named Soundra Lee Johnson. They had a kid and named him Collis Benton Temple, III and then two years later they had another kid named Elliott Lee Temple then hoping for a girl another boy came and he was named Garrett Bartholomew Temple. Soundra and Collis Temple now own two successful businesses. I am proud to be a Temple boy. I hope to follow in the footsteps of my parents. I hope to be successful like both of them. I am proud to be a part of a new generation of Temples.

My brothers and I were easily what you could call privileged, but despite me having everything I needed and most of what I wanted, we were taught a solid value system that has been the foundation for all of our lives. The value of hard work; the qualities of respecting people, leading people, and helping those who may not be able to help themselves; and the ability to maintain a single-minded focus were all things that I learned early on from both of my parents. I was extremely fortunate. I say I was fortunate not so much because of the socioeconomic circumstances that I was raised in, but because of the awareness and understanding that my parents had to make sure I stayed grounded in my community. They were careful to instill in me the sense of pride in my heritage and legacy—a legacy not only as a black man, but also as a member of my family specifically.

I have always been an extremely proud person. Not a conceited pride, but a humble confidence, if there is such a thing, was definitely something instilled in me by my parents, grandparents, and family in general. I remember being nine years old and feeling sorry for the blacks in my class who seemed to want to hang out only with their white class-mates and shunned their black classmates. I still do feel sorry for the African Americans who verbalize a desire to be white or make state-ments insinuating that their lives would probably be better or easier if they were white. That has never been my mentality. My mentor in busi-ness, aside from my father, has always said that I had the "street smarts" of my dad and the class of my mom. Unfortunately for me, I don't believe that either of those two are totally true, but I do believe I have the tough-ness of both of them, which is why I believe I've been able to accomplish the things I have.

My family's legacy has played a role in the pride I exhibit. I am completely aware that in the African American community as a whole, recognition and knowledge of ancestry are not common commodities. This unfortunate fact undoubtedly explains my fascination with and adoration of the entire *Roots* saga, from the capture of Kunta Kinte in West Africa to the scene of Alex Haley returning to the same land from which his headstrong ancestor was stolen. When I speak of the solid foundation that I have been able to stand on, I'm referring to the heritage and background of my family.

JOHNSON LEGACY

Blaine Savoie, the grandfather of my mother, Soundra, never worked for anyone during his life. His entrepreneurial spirit led him in the direction of having the only black-owned cleaners in the small town of Edgard, Louisiana. Blaine's wife, Beulah Borne Savoie, or "Mom," as most people knew her, was the food service supervisor for Second Ward Elementary, which was the school that all the blacks in the town attended. Mom also had the entrepreneurial bug as well, as she would cook food and sell the plates on the weekends. The Savoies were huge believers in saving money and getting out of debt. Blaine was often heard saying, in reference to his home, "This is Blaine Savoie's house, bought and paid for!" This concept of saving and debt freedom was something that they proudly passed on to their children.

Alma Savoie, my grandmother, was the third of their nine children. De De, as she was called, was taught to be extremely clean and became a phenomenal cook. Alma became a great example of her parents' saving habits, as she was known to save at least 25 percent of everything she made and preached that concept to all of her children. Alma assisted her mother in running the cafeteria and food service department for Second Ward for a living. When it was time for Beulah to retire, her choice for her successor was a simple one—her own daughter, Alma Savoie. Alma, without any prior experience in managing people other than watching her mother, was thrust into a leadership position, which she navigated extremely well for thirty years.

Bartholomew Johnson Jr., my grandfather, was a World War II veteran who was born February 10, 1920. He was an extremely gregarious man who loved life and loved people. He was a phenomenal carpenter and built many of the houses in the town of Edgard. Bartholomew was a sportsman. Bateme, as he was called, was a huge boxing fan and an avid hunter.

My great uncle, McKinley Savoie, was the first black sheriff's deputy in Saint John the Baptist Parish. He was the de facto sheriff on the West Bank of the parish because the actual sheriff lived on the East Bank, and blacks and whites alike called him for everything. McKinley served his community extremely well and used the clout he had to make a significant difference in the lives of many of the young people in the parish by doing all types of things. One of the most well-known things McKinley did was buy a bus and make sure the kids that otherwise may not have had the opportunity to travel were able to travel.

Alma and Bartholomew married in 1944 and began their life together. They had four children, three boys and a girl. The oldest, Cornel, was born in 1944. Cornel was followed by Butch in 1946, and the last of the boys was Bruce, born in 1948. Cornel was the first in the Johnson or Savoie family to attend college, choosing and attending Grambling State University in North Louisiana. Butch, my godfather, chose to attend Southern University in Baton Rouge, and Bruce decided to go straight to work after finishing high school.

The last of De De and Bateme's children was a beautiful baby girl they named Soundra Lee Johnson, born on April 12, 1955. Alma raised Soundra with a mind-set and mentality focused around hard work as a foundation of accomplishment. While the boys did their chores—everything from feeding the hogs, chickens, and dogs to the different household repairs and other carpentry work—Soundra, by age eleven, was already expected to clean the entire house. Her duties included mopping, waxing, and buffing the floors to a high shine as well as cleaning the bathrooms well enough to pass the ultimate inspection from Alma "De De" Johnson. To make extra money during middle and high school, Soundra would iron clothes.

Soundra was also very athletic and extremely competitive. She possessed a mentality of "whatever you can do, I can do better," whether it was athletics, academics, or even climbing trees. That way of thinking was definitely something she passed on to me and my three brothers. Growing up, Soundra was known by those in the small town of Edgard as a tomboy because she was always trying to compete with and outdo the boys. She cheered as a varsity cheerleader in the eighth through twelfth grades, serving as the captain in the tenth and twelfth grades. It was a regular occurrence that she would start for the girls' basketball team and then immediately shower and change into her cheerleading uniform for the following boys' game. My mother loved school and literally had perfect attendance throughout middle and high school, graduating third in her high school class from Second Ward High.

As well as Soundra did in school, her mother, Alma always expected better. Soundra recalled that she could get all As and a B, and her mother would ask, "Why didn't you get straight As?" This pursuit and expectation of excellence has remained a staple of my mother's. She did learn as she raised my brothers and me to focus on the good and push us to improve, but I knew she expected excellence in anything I got involved with. As a result, that expectation was something that I began expecting of myself.

During the summers of her eighth-, ninth-, and tenth-grade years, Soundra's mother, Alma, had her attend Straight's Business School in New Orleans. At Straight's summer enrichment program, Soundra learned several business skills that would serve her extremely well during her life. Among many things, she learned accounting, shorthand, and typing. Straight College, which was the precursor of Dillard University, played an educational role on both sides of my family.

After graduating from high school, my mother followed her brother Butch and enrolled at Southern University and A&M College. Southern University has been one of the greatest historically black colleges and universities (HBCUs) in the country for a long time. It's been a mainstay nationally in the African American community for over 135 years. My approach to my college career was adopted from both of my parents, but my mother was extremely instrumental because she earned a degree in business education from Southern in three and a half years. Her accomplishing what she did in college gave me the belief that I could do the same thing. Soundra would sneak and add more classes to her schedule, taking twenty-one hours some semesters, which was beyond what Southern normally would allow. During the summers she would add classes as soon as she could, taking eleven hours whenever possible during the summers. She graduated in December of 1975. Soundra met the man she would ultimately marry in 1974 while she was at Southern and he was starring for LSU.

Upon graduation, Soundra originally planned on opening a boutique clothing store, but instead moved back to her hometown, Edgard, Louisiana. Although she stayed in Edgard for only six months, she was given a job as a teacher on her second day back in the town. She enjoyed teaching, but she knew it was not her calling—neither was small-town life. She wanted to move back to Baton Rouge, and in May 1976, she did so, taking a job working at Louisiana National Bank. She also worked at Rubenstein clothing store part-time as well as selling real estate. Based on her steadfast work ethic, Soundra purchased her first home at twenty-two years old. Although Soundra enjoyed the house and had started really learning the concept of passive income based on having roommates who virtually paid the bills of the house for her, she wouldn't live in that house for very long. It would only be a year later that she would marry and move in with her husband, Collis B. Temple Jr.

TEMPLE LEGACY

John Temple was born in 1874. He had three sisters and four brothers. John was a farmer and a utility linesman, and he was a man, like many of the time, of mixed ancestry, having been born to a white man named Jim Temple, who was born in 1830, and a black woman. My father's grandfather, John, farmed in the summer and spring months and returned to his work as a linesman during the fall and winter months, during the early eras of the telegram lines than ran between Louisiana and Illinois. John married Ida Butler Temple, who was born in 1884 in Greensburg, Louisiana. Great-Grandmother Ida was the start of the strong educational baseline that has been a staple of my family today. Ida went to school in Saint Helena Parish and then went on to attend Straight College in New Orleans, which was the forerunner of Dillard University. Ida B.'s father, Benton Butler, where my middle name comes from, started the school in Saint Helena Parish that she attended. Ida was one of four daughters and two sons born to Benton Butler. All of Benton's daughters went to college, and one of his children, Eugene Butler, went to college and law school and went on to become one of the first black lawyers in the state of Texas. Benton Butler was also one of the major landowners in the parish, having owned six hundred acres of land there.

Ida B. started and ran a school during a time when black children went to school for only three months a year. During the spring and summer months, she would teach in Butler Town near Amite, Louisiana. During the fall and winter seasons, she would teach at her own school on Hillsdale Road. Ida also taught Italian immigrants of all ages to read at night because they weren't allowed to attend school with whites.

In 1911 the youngest of the Temple boys was born, Collis Benton Temple. Collis had two older brothers, Oscar, who was four years older, and Fulton, who was two years older. Because he was the youngest, Collis stayed with Ida B. year-round, traveling with her as she taught children all over the parish, which meant he went to school year-round. In the sixth grade, he started going to school in Kentwood, Louisiana. He graduated from high school, the Tangipahoa Parish Colored Training School, in 1931, and then went on to attend Southern University in Baton Rouge, Louisiana. While at Southern, Collis played football and majored in agriculture and education, graduating in 1936. After college he decided to move to Many, Louisiana, to take a position teaching agriculture and coaching. That's where he met the woman he would spend the rest of his life with, Shirley Cross.

Shirley Yarbrough Cross was born in 1913 to Nathaniel James Cross and Josephine Yarbrough. Nathaniel Cross was born in 1884, and Josephine was born in 1899. The two were not married when Josephine had Shirley, but an example of Shirley's persistence and fortitude is shown by the fact that while caring for her father later in his life, she convinced her parents to get married. Nathaniel had already been married twice, but at seventy-five years old, he and Josephine, who was sixty, became the married couple Shirley had always wanted her parents to become while she was growing up. Shirley had two sisters by her mother: Suprena, who lived most of her life in California, and Sumeria, who moved to northern Louisiana and resided in Shreveport. She also had a brother named Cyril from her father's previous marriage.

Nathaniel Cross attended Tuskegee University around 1902. After finishing, he also became an educator, founding his own school. Shirley and Cyril followed in their father's footsteps and attended Tuskegee as well. Cyril moved to Natchitoches, Louisiana, and became the superintendent of the black trade school in Natchitoches, which was a position he proudly served in for over thirty years. Shirley graduated from Tuskegee and decided to move back home to Louisiana, where she became a GEAN supervisor for the parish, moving around and training the teachers on how to effectively teach. She moved to Many, Louisiana, where she met Collis, or, as he was called, C. B. Temple. They were married in 1939.

Collis and Shirley started their family together in 1940 with the birth of their first daughter, Colleen. In 1942, their next child came, a beautiful baby girl they named Elaine. Their first two children were born in Many, but in 1943, Collis accepted a position as the agriculture teacher and coach at Tangipahoa Parish Colored Training School, the school he had attended and graduated from in Kentwood, Louisiana. Shirley was teaching fifth grade before the move, but after the move, they decided it would be best for her to stay home and focus on raising their growing family. In 1944, their third child was born, another girl, and the woman who would eventually become one of my godmothers, Sandra. In 1946 and 1948, Shirley and Collis had two more girls, Valeria and Brenda, bringing the Temple family to seven, with Collis totally outnumbered by the women of his life. He taught and coached from 1943 to 1950 before being named principal in 1950. On being named principal, Collis made the decision to change the name of the school. Several suggestions were on the table, and people wanted to name the school Lincoln—after the nation's sixteenth president, Abraham Lincoln, who signed the Emancipation Proclamation—or Washington, after the nation's first president. Collis had different thoughts, and in an extremely bold move, almost unheard of at the time, he named the school O. W. Dillon High School, after the man who was his predecessor and who had been principal while he had attended the school. This was such a controversial decision because there were no schools named after a black man in the area.

Collis played a major role in the organizing body of black educators, teachers, and principals in the state of Louisiana, the LIALO, as the chairman of the region for the Florida and Feliciana Parishes of Louisiana, starting in 1950. He had a great relationship with and was extremely close to

J. K. Haynes, who was the head of the Black Teachers Organization and a de facto superintendent of black education in the state. While attending an organization meeting in November of 1952, with a pregnant wife and five girls at home, he was called out of the meeting. It is said that on his return, with sweat on his forehead, he shouted with pride (and a sigh of relief), "I finally got my boy!" Collis Benton Temple Jr. was born on November 8, 1952.

Between 1950 and 1954, Collis Temple Sr. unsuccessfully tried to attend Louisiana State University several times to obtain his master's degree. Due to the intense racial climate at the time, he was not allowed to attend. Louisiana's state legislature actually appropriated funds for Collis to attend Michigan State University rather than allowing him to attend the flagship school for higher education in the state. In 1956 Collis graduated from Michigan State with his master's degree. Shirley would follow and earn her master's from Atlanta University in 1965. In 1968, Shirley, along with Collis's support, made the bold decision, as a black woman in the Deep South, to run for state representative. She lost a hard-fought and extremely close race by only 106 total votes to an Italian American named Anzalone. Collis also tried his hand at politics with two bids at the state senate in 1972 and 1976, earning a spot in the runoff both times before losing to Bill Dykes in both instances.

C. B. and Shirley were big believers in education, family (they remained married for over fifty-five years until Collis's death in 1995), and a strong work ethic. My father says he always saw his parents working as a team, and that's what he wanted to have. The Temples also had an entrepreneurial spirit, as Collis Sr. had four incomes that he brought into the Temple household. C. B. sold black history encyclopedias to all of the schools he oversaw, as well as anyone who found value in the knowledge. His salary as principal of the high school was the main source of income, but as an agricultural teacher, C. B. could butcher cattle and can the meat. As the chairman of the region for the LIALO, he would offer his services over the weekend to go to Manchac to pick up fish and sell it to the schools. Every school in C. B.'s region would enjoy fish on Mondays and canned meat later during the week. Also, understanding the value of passive income, C. B. owned rental property and served as a landlord as well as owning several tractors. He would have work done and pay those who drove the tractors for him for the job or by the hour.

Growing up, Collis Jr. had a strong work ethic instilled in him. As early as age nine, he would have to wake up between 4:30 a.m. and 5:00 a.m. to go take care of the two calves and four hogs that he had been given responsibility to care for. He was expected to feed and water them every morning, and had to make the half-mile trek in the dark most mornings. From the fourth grade to the tenth grade, Collis took part in the 4-H club and would show calves. He got a taste of earning his own money early on in life. While in the fifth grade at ten years old, his calf was named Reserve Champion, and he earned $950 for the calf. It was at that point when he first developed his outlook that HARD WORK PAYS OFF! In the seventh grade, Collis sold two calves at one event, earning $2,200 for a first-place winner and $800 for another winner that day, bringing his total earnings to $3,000 for the day. The summer after his seventh-grade year, he had a bank account with about $1,500 in it and bought a Honda 65 motorcycle. Obviously, he was too young to LEGALLY drive it, but he grew up in the country, and he was bigger than most kids his age. It was important to C. B. and Shirley to shield their children as they grew up from any type of situation where they would be made to feel less than the best or made to feel like second-class citizens in any way. Because of the respect people had for Collis Sr. around the small town of Kentwood, among both blacks and whites, C. B. was called Mr. Temple or Reverend, even though he wasn't a pastor, and he had no problem looking at white men eye to eye, which was not a normal happening at the time in the Deep South. My grandfather was always well dressed and was a proud man who respected those who respected him and focused on hard work and results. That was the example that was set by Collis Sr. for my father, Collis Jr.

Collis Jr., although mischievous, was a great student, and he had added incentive considering he was taught English by his mother, and he attended the school where his father was principal. Very similarly to my own upbringing, my father always had everything he needed and was allowed to EARN anything he wanted. He and his sisters grew up well, and the Temple family was extremely well respected, not just in Kentwood, but all over the state. Collis, or Booster, which he was affectionately called by those closest to him, excelled in every sport he played—track and field, football, and basketball—winning the state championship in football and playing for the championship in basketball before losing his senior year. When we watched the Denzel Washington movie *Remember the Titans*, my father would just shake his head, smile, and say, "I remember going through all of that for real!" His senior year, in 1969, the schools were integrated, and that was his first real experience at close range with white people on a daily basis, other than dealing with them under controlled circumstances for short periods of time. O. W. Dillon became the middle school, as did all of the black high schools in the area, and the white schools became the high schools. The difference in my father's situation from *Remember the Titans* was that the white coach became the head coach, as with most of the schools in the Deep South. Along with that change came a similar crippling of the power base of many areas in Louisiana. Pastors, teachers, principals, doctors, and attorneys were the most prominent and respected positions in the African American community. Although integration was extremely necessary, it somewhat broke down the power structure of the black administrators and educators in the South during the 1970s.

My grandfather's decision to not only allow but to encourage my father to integrate Louisiana State University's basketball team was a MONUMENTAL decision of epic proportions because of the ripple effect that it had and the lives that it impacted, directly and indirectly. In 1969 when my father was being recruited, there was no such thing as an National Collegiate Athletic Association violation prohibiting someone like the governor of a state from being involved in the recruiting process of an athlete. To shed some light on the enormity of my father's potential decision to integrate a major sport at LSU, think about the fact that the governor of Louisiana in 1969, Fox McKeithan, called

Collis Sr. and asked him to strongly consider sending my father to LSU. It should be clarified that under the circumstances, the assimilation of an African American onto LSU's basketball team was about much more than just an ability to play the game of basketball. The decision was one that HAD to work; otherwise the opportunity to break the color barrier may have very well been pushed back several more years. The decision on the RIGHT person for the move to be made was critically important. It related to his understanding of social issues and how to handle them; his upbringing and life experiences; his support system; his intelligence, intellect, and ability to compete in the classroom; and, last, his ability to compete and excel on the field of play, the basketball court.

Collis B. Temple Jr. made the decision to sign with LSU and made history. He attended LSU and majored in general business. During the early 1970s, freshman athletes were still not allowed to play with the varsity team. Collis starred for Press Maravich's freshman Tiger team. Press Maravich was not only LSU's basketball coach, but also the man who brought his son, the legendary "Pistol" Pete Maravich, to LSU with him. He was also, fittingly so, a man who had always seen, even in the early 1950s, that the future of basketball was one of colorblindness, where athletes of all ethnicities played alongside one another as teammates and against one another in competition. During his sophomore campaign, Collis immediately became a starter on the varsity squad and remained a starter for the rest of his career. After being recruited and coached for two years by Press Maravich, Collis played his last two seasons for the legendary LSU basketball coach Dale Brown.

While at LSU, Collis dealt with a great deal of racial challenges. Those challenges came from all angles: from opposing fans and players around the country, especially the Deep South; fellow students; professors; academic advisors; trainers; and even, in certain instances, his own teammates. I think about my dad's viewpoint as a seventeen- and eighteen-year-old on LSU's campus with very few people around him—other than the janitors and cafeteria workers—who looked like him and could relate to him. The janitors and cafeteria workers around the campus became some of my dad's friends and confidants as he fought the battle, oftentimes a mental one, to blaze a trail for future generations.

When Collis got to LSU and decided that he wanted to take the amount and type of courses necessary to ensure his graduation in four years with a quality degree, his academic advisor sneered and said, "Nigger, I'll be coming to watch you play at Southeastern next year. You'll flunk out. You'll never pass fifteen hours at LSU." That academic advisor actually went on to serve in the state legislature in Louisiana. Notwithstanding all the death threats and hate mail that would come on a regular basis, Collis engaged in verbal battles in LSU's free-speech alley with a man who would serve in Louisiana as a state senator and, sadly enough, would even earn a spot in the runoff for governor of Louisiana, David Duke. Duke was at LSU at the same time as Collis, and the eventual Grand Wizard of the Ku Klux Klan was at no loss for words. Neither was Collis. Then there was the death threat at Vanderbilt, where a letter was sent to the locker room at halftime saying that if Temple returned to play in the second half, it would be the last half of basketball that he would play. During that trying situation, Dale Brown reiterated the seriousness of the matter to Collis while in the visitor's locker room, but Collis decided that because the letter hadn't been signed, the person was obviously a coward. He was absolute in his decision to finish the game. There was no attempt on his life, and LSU was victorious in the game.

Although the challenges that he faced while at LSU were many, Collis also built phenomenal lifetime relationships with several of his teammates, classmates, coaches, and administrators. He endeared himself to almost all LSU fans who watched the games and were inspired by his heart, loyalty, work ethic, and staying power, despite the seemingly insurmountable odds stacked against his eventual success. He was a First Team Academic All-Southeastern Conference Honor Roll recipient during the 1972–1973 season, as well as an All-SEC Selection during his senior year, 1973–1974. He graduated from LSU with a degree in kinesiology in 1974. Collis also went on to earn his master's degree from LSU.

After an All-SEC career at LSU and a senior season that saw Collis average a double-double, he was drafted by National Basketball Association, American Basketball Association, and even National Football League teams (based on his size, agility, and athleticism, he was drafted as a receiver). He played professionally for just over three years with the San Antonio Spurs and Seattle Supersonics, and even had a short stint overseas in Spain before returning to Baton Rouge permanently to start his life at the urging of his father, who told him, "It's time for you to put that ball down and go to work, boy."

While playing ball, Collis would spend his time during the off-season doing everything from studying for and earning his real estate license to wisely spending his money on purchasing and fixing up rental houses. Collis, in addition to his rental income, also started working with the newly elected mayor in Baton Rouge, Pat Screen, a man whom he had gone to college with and who was a quarterback for the Tiger football team while they had been in college together. Collis took a job running the youth development program for the city of Baton Rouge. The job put him in the forefront from a community-involvement standpoint, and his lifetime of community service began. He and Soundra also decided to start the company that they would grow together into a massive success, helping thousands of people all over the state of Louisiana in an assortment of ways. The Harmony Center became a staple in the Baton Rouge community and soon began to spread throughout Louisiana. Collis's relationship with Soundra also grew stronger, and on September 16, 1978, they were married.

WSTM LESSONS LEARNED

1. Never take for granted the sacrifices and the work that was done for you to experience whatever success you may be experiencing now.
2. As tough as the challenges you're going through may be, some-one has dealt with and overcome situations and circumstances that were tougher than yours! Remember that and press on. Don't ever play the "woe is me..." game.
3. Value and be grateful for your foundation, and if you were not blessed to have a great one, CREATE ONE!

Chapter 2

A NEW GENERATION OF TEMPLES

*Unless there's a change in programming, it's tough
for someone who's only watched people WAIT
for a check to compete with someone who's
watched people WORK for a check!
It's all about PROGRAMMING and
REPROGRAMMING! —Collis Temple III*

With Collis and Shirley Temple having had only one son, and me being my father's first child and the namesake of both my grandfather and father, I have always felt, right or not, as if I was the unofficial torchbearer of the Temple name. With all the people that the family has impacted in a positive way and everything that the Temples have accomplished, I always felt that representing them to the best of my ability was of the utmost importance.

I had many talented cousins, most of whom were older, considering the fact that my dad was the youngest and the last to start having children. I looked up to several of them. I can remember loving to go to Franklinton, Louisiana, with my cousins Lorren, Ladette, and Lyle Magee. Their older brother, Lance, was out of the house by the time I was old enough to start going with other family members for extended periods of time. Aunt Colleen and Uncle George were great, and I remember thinking how proud I was as we would drive up to their house amid the cornfields in Franklinton, thinking, "This is the biggest and nicest house on the street—my family has it going on all over the place!" I remember the red carpet in their family room, the tile floors in the kitchen and living room, and the fact that they had an upstairs, which I was amazed by at the time (our parents hadn't renovated our home to the point where we had an upstairs yet)! Aunt Colleen was my grandparents' first child and always made sure that everyone knew it! I vividly remember the excitement from those trips and the bonds that I built with Ladette and especially with Lorren. Lorren is eleven years older than I am and always looked out for me and my brothers. That trait persisted all the way through both my and my younger brother's college basketball careers, when she and Ladette would be quick to defend us if someone had anything to say that wasn't favorable about their "little cousins'" performances, as they called us. Lorren is someone who has shown me the importance of family remaining close and staying in contact. Lorren also followed in the footsteps of my great-grandmother Ida B. in her choice to attend and graduate from Dillard University in New Orleans.

Another set of cousins I admired a great deal was the Tulls. Uncle Knox and Aunt Brenda, who was the youngest girl and directly before my father, were inspirations as well. Their success in business was amazing to me, only to be surpassed by my admiration for the way their family seemed to always have it together. Uncle Knox and Aunt Brenda decided to name their children after African kings and queens, as you can tell by their names: Mossi, Nzinga, Kimathi, and Hapshetsu (aka: Happy). They were so much fun to be around. To a great extent, a part of the pride I had about African American history came from them as a family. They lived in Washington, DC, and while we didn't get to see them a lot, it was a big deal every few years when we did. I remember listening to Mossi and Kimathi talking about the company their father had helped cofound, Jackson & Tull, and the work that they had helped do on the

Manhattan Bridge and the Hubble Telescope. I would think, "They are working in arenas that affect the entire world!" Looking at the fun they always seemed to be having in family photos and spending time with them was once again another example to me of how important that family unit is. When Mossi went off to college at Morehouse in Atlanta, he would often bring friends to Baton Rouge before they went to New Orleans and spend time with our family. I remember that I could listen to Mossi talk all night long about our family legacy, politics, or whatever else he felt like talking about. I actually decided my college major based on a conversation with him. The choice was economics, but once I realized what that entailed, I made the practical choice for me and switched to general business.

I learned several things from a few of my cousins, but Lorren and Mossi have impacted me the most. As part of the next generation of Temples, they were people early in my life who were close to my age and made a difference. When Lorren opened her boutique, I remember that she had a picture of my grandfather behind the cash register in her store. To this day, Mossi has the original card in his wallet that my grandfather had as a member of the National Association Advancement of Colored People (NAACP). These two people, I believe, are great examples of the next generation of Temples.

"You can't get ahead stayin' in bed! Time to get up! The early bird gets the worm! Let's go!" This is what I would hear as my dad would shake me awake in the mornings. Saturday morning cartoons were a staple for most kids when my brother Elliott and I were growing up in the 1980s and 1990s, but I can remember that we didn't have the chance to engage in the stimulating dialogue of the *Smurfs, He-Man, Thundercats, Tom and Jerry*, and the like. For as long as I can remember, we were getting up pretty early, between 6:00 a.m. and 6:30 a.m. on Saturdays, and going with Dad to paint a house, strip some cypress wood of nails so we could recycle and reuse the wood, move a house, or give the crew the working orders for the day. The best part of those Saturday mornings, in addition to the time spent talking to Dad and learning life lessons, was the fact that, following the work, an unbelievable breakfast would be waiting for us back home. Mom's cooking usually included pancakes, bacon, grits, and sausage. That was the schedule on Saturday mornings for the most part, and unless we were in season and had a game or meet based on whatever sport we were in at that time of year, the schedule didn't deviate a whole lot. The time spent around the kitchen table was priceless, and whether it was breakfast on Saturday morning or dinner most days of the week, those conversations helped set the framework for the rest of my life.

My brothers and I all have distinctively different personalities, ways of thinking and acting, and ways that we think about certain things, but despite the fact that we do things differently, the foundation that we've grown from has helped put all three of us in a position of success in life because we all enjoy where we are in life as we strive to do and become more. Garrett, the youngest, has accomplished what was a lifelong dream of mine—and I think of his as well—as he plays in the NBA. At the time of this book, he was playing as a backup guard with the Washington Wizards. Elliott, the brother directly under me, is currently working with my father in business and is really finding and creating his niche in real estate and as a developer.

Like any brothers growing up, we got in fights with each one another and got into trouble every once in a while, but nothing major—probably from the fear of being whipped by our parents. For the most part, we really got along and had a great relationship. Elliott, who is two years younger than I am, and I would compete at things all the time. Elliott has always looked older than me and been built more solidly than me. That was tough to deal with early on because everyone would always think he was the oldest, and I took great pride in being the oldest son to the only male child of Collis and Shirley Temple. Elliott and I would only fight when it came to some type of competition. I guess it started pretty early on, because my mom comically reminds me of when I was two years old and Elliott had just been born. A ritual was for my mom to read me a book to put me to bed every night, and it seems that Elliott's birth threw a kink in the rotation. My mom recalls me saying, "I can't stand that ole' baby, hunh!" As we grew up, I really started taking pride in having a little brother and playing the big-brother role, but as Elliott started outgrowing me, running faster than me, and looking older than me, the competition started to grow. Because he was always stronger than me since I can remember, and overpowering him physically quickly became out of the question (I tried that a few times with no success), the only way I could beat him was on the basketball court. My first recollection of competition was competing with Elliott. There is absolutely no doubt in my mind that Elliott helped me not only become the athlete I eventually ended up becoming, but, much more important, the man I am today. I always wanted to be a great example for him and Garrett. I always wanted them to see me as their older brother who set the bar high and expected them to meet it.

My brother Garrett and I had a different relationship than Elliott and I did. I was again the big brother, but I think I had a different role. We are seven years apart. When it came to Garrett, if I wasn't playing peacekeeper between him and Elliott, I was usually Garrett's favorite toy! I really believe that early on, Garrett's thought was that I was his toy to be used at his discretion. Whether it was playing basketball (and occasionally letting him win every one out of ten, which probably didn't help matters) or playing a game of one-on-one tackle football in my parents' bedroom because it was the biggest, Garrett and I spent a lot of time together.

The toughest time I believe I've endured with my brothers was dealing with our parents' separation and subsequent divorce. The separation took place when I was a seventeen-year-old junior in high school, Elliott was a fifteen-year-old freshman, and Garrett was a ten-year-old middle schooler. My way of dealing with any tough situation was ignoring it and going to the gym and shooting for hours—I loved it, and it was my escape. Elliott had a hard time dealing with the divorce as well, because so much of his identity was built around us being a family. He's still like that today; that's why I believe he's such a great husband and a great father to his twins, Kyndall and Elliott Jr. Garrett easily had the toughest time dealing with the divorce, mainly because he was the youngest and, at the end of the day, had to be in the middle of all of it for the longest period of time. When it happened he didn't have much to say, but you could see the difference in him in his TOTALLY independent way of thinking. My mother was constantly preaching to us about being independent thinkers, and both Elliott and I became independent thinkers in that we never followed the crowd or worried about what may have been popular from the standpoint of our peers. Today we both are independent thinkers and have strong and decisive beliefs. That being said, even today, neither Elliott nor I will make any major decisions without at least running the idea by our parents. Garrett took my mother's concept of independent thinking to another level. He MAY ask their opinion, but simply for perspective. I admire Garrett for his strength and independence. I was seventeen and a year and a half from moving out for good when my parents separated. Elliott had to deal with it for three and a half years, but Garrett had to split time for eight years. I know it was tough, but he did it.

Watching Garrett taught me that there's definitely more than one way to do things. I'm reminded of several instances; both happened during Garrett's redshirt freshman year at LSU. The first was when LSU media day came around, and Garrett had picked the number he wanted to wear. Under most conditions this really isn't a big deal, but it was to me based on the circumstances. I had just finished my career at LSU a few years earlier, having worn the number forty-one, which also happened to be the number my dad wore at LSU while he played. Garrett had worn number forty-one while in high school, and I really liked the idea of him paying honor to our father as I had by wearing number forty-one in college as well. Garrett had different thoughts and decided to switch the number around and wear number fourteen. He was determined to blaze his own trail, and even though I didn't agree at the time, I realized that it wasn't my decision to make and learned to respect him for his independent reasoning and decision making. A couple of weeks into his freshman year, I asked Garrett how he was enjoying his college experience and if he was practicing a lot and working on his game. I reminded him that I had worked really hard during my basketball career, waking up early, putting up hundreds of extra jumpers daily, always taking pride in being at practice first and being the last to leave. Garrett promptly told me, "I'm not you!" I was blown away, but I truly realized at that moment that Garrett was his own man and was definitely going to do things his own way. That was literally the last time I gave Garrett any unsolicited advice. He ended up starting all four years at LSU after his redshirt year. His redshirt freshman year, Garrett stood out as a defensive stopper and major cog in the team's success. During the team's unbelievable Final Four run his first year, Garrett led the team in minutes played and averaged per game during the entire NCAA Tournament at over forty minutes per game! That's so unbelievable because college basketball games are only forty minutes long. (The over-forty-minute average came as a result of an overtime game.) What else is impressive about that number is that some of the other players on that Final Four team were superstars, like senior leading scorer and team captain Darrell Mitchell (who was a freshman contributor when I was a senior at LSU); Tasmin Mitchell, who was a true freshman and had just been named a McDonald's All-American the year before and earned a spot on the All-SEC Freshman Team that year; Glen Davis, who was SEC Player of the Year as a sophomore that year and was fresh off of his SEC Freshman of the Year campaign, and Tyrus Thomas, who had reluctantly redshirted the year before with Garrett and, due to his great play and ridiculous athleticism, had subsequently burst on the national scene that year, catapulting him to the honor of SEC Freshman of the Year that year and to the number-two pick in the draft after that summer. Today, LSU's first seven from that team have played professionally, and two other than Garrett play in the NBA. Despite the fact that he's become a nice scorer, while at LSU he didn't reach the lauded "1,000 Point Club," but he left his mark all over the LSU record books. When he graduated he had played more minutes than any player in LSU history! When I attended Garrett's first NBA game as a Houston Rocket, try as I did, I couldn't keep from crying because, whether it was right or wrong, I felt like all the hard work I had put in had paid off through him. I was so excited for him, and

I remembered all of the one-on-one games and the encouragement I gave him as a middle and high schooler. Garrett currently plays for the Washington Wizards and has been on the team for four years. He's in his sixth year in the NBA and has built a great career. I am extremely proud of him, and the best part is that he's done it his way.

I totally respect those who are the trailblazers of a new path in their families, such as those who were the first to graduate from high school or college in their families. But that wasn't our story, and despite the fact that we were taught that earning a degree didn't promise you anything and that business ownership was the only way to go when it came to life after college, it was still important to uphold a legacy. Both Elliott and Garrett earned their degrees and, much more important, are constructive members of society. They are leaders of men and women in their own right and way. It's a great feeling to be a part of a new generation of Temples.

WSTM LESSONS LEARNED

1. Take pride in who you are. You may be the person who has to start the legacy-creation process in your family, or it may be your charge to take a family legacy to the next level. Whatever the situation, accept the challenge!
2. Remember to be a 360° learner. You can learn from everyone. Learn from others' experiences. Some may be great examples and some may not be the greatest examples, but do your best to take every example and encounter as an opportunity to learn and grow.

Chapter 3

LEARNING TO COMPETE AND LEAD

*Play hard. Value relationships. Be loyal. Give
100 percent in everything you do.
And compete...above all, COMPETE! —Gregg Popovich*

Leadership is EVERYTHING! —Art Williams

There have been so many different instances in my life where I have had the phenomenal opportunity to experience what President Barack Obama has called "teachable moments" in relation to learning the value of competition and leadership. Being a parent and seeing how much of my first daughter's mental capacity and personality is developed early in her life, I marvel at how much these early lessons have actually impacted my overall thought process and shaped my life as it is today.

I remember being barely six or seven years old and asking my father why the employees who worked for him and my mother at the Harmony Center worked for them and did not make the decision to go start their own businesses like he and my mom had. The answer was simple and to the point, and I remember it to this day: "Because they think like EMPLOYEES and not BUSINESS OWNERS, Collis. Those are two different ways of thinking." As long ago as that was and as succinct of an answer as he gave, it has always stayed with me, and, based on that, I knew I wanted to become a leader of people, an entrepreneur, and a winner.

Leadership, in my mind, was a major part of winning. From my earliest recollections, I always said that I was going to be an NBA basketball player and a businessman. I would daydream about playing in the NBA and then leaving the game with a suit on and a briefcase in hand, heading to go take care of business. I honestly had no idea what "business" I was heading to take care of, but a confident, handsome, well-groomed business man was the image I had in my mind. I was fortunate to have a real-life example of exactly that every day in my father. I was also extremely fortunate to have a mother who exemplified hard work, a competitive spirit, and compassion, all wrapped in a beautiful package. When people say that many men look for a woman like their mother, I can vividly remember thinking as a young man that I'd be in great shape if I was able to find someone like my mom! The things we aspire to become are not so amazing when we take the time to think about the examples we see on a regular basis and the things we base those aspirations on.

BIDDY BASKETBALL, AAU, AND THE SPORTS ACADEMY

The earliest lesson about competition and leadership that I can really remember came as a six-year-old on the first organized basketball team that I played on. I was in the first grade, and as with most of the early teams I played on, my dad was the coach. As I think back, it was a great thing that my dad was the coach, because that experience could have turned out a lot differently. I don't remember a lot from that first team, but there are a few things that I still remember and that stand out to me. One, we wore gray uniforms; two, I wasn't very good; and, last, a guy who later became a great friend and teammate of mine, Troy Williams, was the best player on the team, by far! Now you may be thinking, how do you remember who was the best player on a six-year-old Biddy Ball league team nearly thirty years later? Easy, it was that obvious! I don't remember much from that first year of organized play, but I can still recall that it was the first time that I was made to believe by my dad that I should play point guard. According to him, that was the person who led the team. I remember being aware that Troy was the best player on the team, but I can also remember deciding that I wanted to get better and in essence close the gap between us. Even though I wasn't the best player, I realized even at six years old that Troy couldn't do everything, and he'd need some help. I started working on my ball handling at home in the driveway every once in a while. In six-year-old Biddy Ball, there are no real positions. The "point guard" is usually just the person who dribbles the ball up the court, but I took pride in being the leader, and although I had a lot more to learn about leadership, I can remember that incident being the first understanding of what being a leader was about. Looking back now, having become much more perceptive and astute regarding leadership principles, my mind-set about leadership early on was a lot more closely tied to what the leadership expert John Maxwell calls "positional leadership." "I'm the point guard, so I'm the leader!"—but at least it was a start.

The next year, I was a second grader; things were different. I had improved by leaps and bounds. I was playing on two different teams. Once again my dad coached BOTH teams. One was a school team that was made up of members of my class at school. We played at the YMCA, in a very nice facility called A. C. Lewis. The second team I played on that year was in what is called the Baton Rouge Recreation Commission (BREC) league and was played at a gym named Anna T. Jordan, which I would say was not as nice of a facility as the A. C. Lewis YMCA.

There were a couple of other distinct differences. In the YMCA league, they didn't formally keep the score. They didn't call things as tightly in terms of enforcement of the rules, like traveling and other things. This was the year that my real competitive streak started to develop. We'd play a game in the YMCA league and murder the team, and after the game, as we were walking by the other team and giving them handshakes and high fives in a show of sportsmanship, I'd hear the other coach—probably a father as well—saying something to the effect of, "Good game, we're all winners." I never liked that and oftentimes would make a point to quickly remind the other players on the opposing team of what the score was at the game's end and how badly we had beat them. I would remind them that there could be only one real winner and that it was definitely us! Making it known that we were the clear-cut winner was something that I took great pride in.

Traveling across town to my next game in the BREC league on those Saturday mornings at Anna T. Jordan, I knew I'd never have to deal with the same issues we had in the YMCA league. It was a totally different atmosphere. First of all, the YMCA league was more racially mixed, whereas the BREC league was predominately (99 percent if I had to guess) black. Another major difference when heading across town was the difference in parental support. Although there were always parents present at the BREC games, they did not show up in as large a quantity as they did to the YMCA games. I truly realized even at an early age that it was different that I had a dad who was coaching me and a mother who NEVER missed a game. Mom was extremely knowledgeable, and her competitive spirit was easily on par with my dad's. She was always there and was usually the loudest voice in the stands. The competition level was a lot higher, and there were only a few times where I dominated these games to the extent that I did in the YMCA league. In the BREC league, not only did they keep score, but there was a huge scoreboard on the wall above the court that let everyone in the gym know who was winning and by how much. The only time they would turn off the scoreboard was when one team was up by more than twenty points! I can remember instances when our team was on both ends of the scoreboard. It only happened once or twice where we had the "scoreboard busted" or "twenty-point ruled" on us, but it was extremely embarrassing and left a nasty taste in my mouth and mind about losing. I also remember the killer instinct in me wanting to bust the scoreboard on other teams and striving to almost embarrass them. This was not something that my dad pushed as much one way or another, but I always knew he wanted to win as well. Dad was always big on winning, but his mind-set was that there was definitely a classy way to do it, and the most important thing was simply playing the best that you possibly could. He wasn't about embarrassing teams, and he was always big on sportsmanship when we lost and especially when we won, which happened much more often.

Playing in the BREC league at Anna T. Jordan helped me start to see that things were different from a socioeconomic standpoint. Having been raised under a privileged set of circumstances, playing in that league— along with my almost daily visits to the Sports Academy—truly gave me insight into a world that was different than the one I was being raised in. As I mentioned earlier, my parents had started a company the year before I was born that was called the Harmony Center. They started out with one home for juvenile delinquent boys. The Harmony Center has grown by leaps and bounds over the last thirty-plus years, but during the early years of the business, my father also worked as the head of the youth development program for the mayor at the time, Pat Screen. My father led the initiative to transform what was an old gym for firefighters near downtown Baton Rouge into a community gym that became known as the Sports Academy. It has since been renamed the Lester Roberts Sports Academy for the man whom my father and the LSU basketball coach and college basketball coaching legend of the time, Dale Brown, got to come down to Baton Rouge from New York to run the gym, Lester Roberts.

Lester started off working at the Harmony Center and running the Sports Academy. Before long, he began making the Sports Academy a household name in Baton Rouge, producing phenomenal sports programs and summer camps as well as mentoring countless children, especially African American young men, and helping hundreds of boys take advantage of the opportunity to go to college through using sports as an avenue. The Sports Academy would also serve, among many others things, as a safe haven for some of the boys at the Harmony Center to go to and experience healthy competition, serving as a substitute for potentially detrimental activity. "The Academy," as many people called it, became my home away from home. Looking back over my life, when I really assess things, the Sports Academy played a huge role in helping me develop as a competitor. I remember everything—from having to earn my respect beyond just being "Collis Temple's son" to playing with the older guys and having them knock me around and rough me up. While I was growing up, the Sports Academy introduced a league, still in operation today, called the House League. The competition was amazing, and there are actually at least five currently active NBA players who participated in the House League games while growing up.

Amateur Athletic Union (AAU) basketball was a world that I was introduced to at a young age as well, around ten or eleven. My father was my coach most of the time, with the exception of one or two years. It came the same time every year. The start of the season was near the end of the school year in March and went throughout the summer. There were many lessons learned during those summers of endless basketball and higher-level competition. I see people who coach their kids and give their kids the upper hand when it comes to having to compete for positions. My father never did that. I guess he understood that I was going to take a bunch of mess anyway, and that maybe it would be cut back if I had truly earned the spot. As a result of my father's mentality about me EARNING my spot, I didn't start for my own dad's AAU team until I was thirteen years old. That was three years of having to come off of the bench most of the time. I remember Dad explaining to me the reasoning for him handling the situation the way he did. It made such great sense that I always believed he had my best interest at heart and really never questioned his motives. I vividly remember when I earned the starting point guard spot for good and the circumstances surrounding that occurrence. We were playing a really good team, and the guy who was starting at point guard at the time, Damarius Atkins, had copped an attitude about something that had been done during the previous game. I got my chance and played extremely well. We won the game, and that was that. I had been playing well before then, coming off the bench, but Damarius, who was a better athlete than I was at the time, hadn't done anything to lose his spot in the starting lineup. My dad would just tell me that my chance would come and to be ready. "The cream always rises to the top, Collis," is what he would constantly tell me. Thinking back on it, it's really funny, because with him being the team's head coach, he could have just given me the starting spot at any time. That was his way of teaching; it was always about the lessons and making sure that I EARNED it. This was the first experience where I realized that if I stayed the course and continued doing the right things, my opportunities would present themselves, and I would have the chance to take advantage of them and experience the success that I wanted. Although we won a few state AAU titles, we never really got any major national recognition like some of the teams my dad coached later on did. Nevertheless, my experience playing AAU basketball was yet another instance in the building of my competitive fortitude and mentality.

I learned several leadership lessons while playing for my father, but a few that I can remember extremely well came in the form of sportsmanship and overall integrity, character, and honesty. You may ask, "How did these stick out more so than some of the others?" The answer probably lies in the physicality with which these lessons were taught and learned. I'll explain what I mean by *physicality*. My sixth-grade school team was "playing up" in a seventh-grade tournament at a local gym, and after a hard-fought battle, we ended up losing to a really good team in a close game. I was extremely disappointed, so much so that as we walked off of the court, I followed the lead of a hot-tempered teammate of mine who happened to be walking only a few steps ahead of me. He ripped his jersey off in a fury and threw it to the ground. (Before I go any further, I probably need to mention that this was a Caucasian kid who, although a good athlete, had a tendency to have a quick temper. Even today, the young man's father and my father have a good relationship because of the discipline my dad helped instill in the young man at a young age.) The game hadn't been over for five seconds, and before doing the good-sportsmanship and gentlemanly move of shaking hands with the other team's members as I normally would, I was about to follow him in pulling my jersey off and throwing it to the ground in a demonstration of just how mad I was about the loss. As I started to pull the jersey off, I felt something hit the back of my head as if someone had thrown a rock out of the fifth row of the stands! I heard, "Boy, what the hell are you doing?" As I somewhat stumbled forward, trying catch my balance, turn around, and at the same time figure out who had hit me, I already knew it was my dad, and I quickly put the jersey back on me in its rightful place. The conversation afterward was that under no circumstances does a leader EVER follow anyone in doing the wrong thing! Dad stressed that I was supposed to be the leader all the time, not just when it was convenient, when we won, and when things were going well. As the LEADER, I was supposed to be SETTING the example, not following the wrong example. He would stress that one of the best opportunities to set an example, despite the fact that it may not have happened as often, was when we lost or things didn't necessarily go the way I may have wanted them to go. I remember there were times when my mom thought that Dad was too hard on me—and I did too sometimes—but to her credit, she allowed the lessons to be taught because of her understanding and hopefulness about the man they would mold me into. The lessons were always clear and always helped me to become better as a person.

There was another situation in the summer of 1995 during fifteen-and-under AAU basketball when, on a road trip, one of my teammates came up with the bright idea to steal the shoes of someone from another team. These were some Jordans, and stealing them was a BIG deal! I actually never saw the shoes, nor did I have anything to do with the plan to steal or the subsequent act of stealing the shoes, but, after the fact, I knew that it had been done and didn't tell my dad. Because of that, I was punished along with the rest of the team. All but only two or three guys were legitimately innocent of any wrongdoing. What was the punishment? Everyone who was involved in any way was lined up in front of the few teammates who weren't involved, as well as all the parents, and paddled with three licks each. The young man who actually stole the shoes got more, because after he got the licks from my dad, he got them from his own parents as well. I really learned several things: First, always do what's right, even when the crowd doesn't. Second, everyone on the team may not be honest and loyal. (One of the guys who had actually tried on the stolen shoes and never admitted it watched us get paddled and never admitted that he had had some major involvement. My dad only paddled the young men who admitted to being involved. I never looked at that guy the same way.) Third, honesty and integrity are always the best options. Just tell the truth.

RUNNING CROSS-COUNTRY AND TRACK

When it came to competing and leading, other areas that grew my competitive spirit and leadership skills a great deal were cross-country and track. I don't remember exactly how it happened, but I remember being in the fifth grade, and my dad somehow got the cross-country coach to let me run with the junior varsity team. Without having personally run cross-country before himself, I have often wondered how my dad made the choice to use it as a tool to build up so many things in me as an athlete and a young man. When I asked my father many years later why he chose cross-country, he stated that he realized I would be pretty good because when I would run around the lakes with him in the fourth grade while he was trying to stay in shape, I was actually able to beat him and just didn't realize it. When I think back about him saying "I just didn't realize it," what he was saying was that my mental toughness hadn't been tested enough for me to understand that I could push through a little pain and drive my body to another level.

My dad admitted to me in secret that track was in fact his favorite sport, but the reality was that he realized I did not have the God-given ability to excel as a sprinter and speedster, and that's where the idea of running long distance came from. My cross-country career started, as I mentioned earlier, while I was in the fifth grade at U-High, and I ran with the junior varsity team. That first year, in 1990 as an eleven-year-old, I ran in four meets. The junior varsity ran a two-mile course, while the varsity ran a three-mile course. I was the best runner on the junior varsity team, running against sixth, seventh, and eighth graders and even some high school freshmen. My best two-mile time that year was 13:10, and I improved every time. I remember learning to focus on just beating the last time I had run. That first year running cross-country, I learned the concept of beating my "personal best," which is a concept that I think would serve a lot of people well in their everyday lives and has served me well over the last twenty-plus years. I really started excelling in the sixth grade.

My dad's uncanny ability to seemingly see into the future and connect the dots before anyone else realized that the dots existed leads me to believe that that was why he had me running cross-country and long distance on the track team at such a young age. He realized early on that I wasn't going to be very strong or very athletic, but that I could excel based on my capacity to push myself and to be mentally tough. He understood that long term, and for the rest of my life, this attribute, mental toughness, would navigate me through many interesting challenges. Thinking back, I realize that it's one thing to spot this, but to then find a situation where I would be able to act on it, excel in it, and build on it makes it that much bigger of a deal.

Running cross-country and summer track with the K-Y Track Club presented a different set of competitive circumstances that I had not dealt with before. I was used to playing basketball and having a team around me (despite the fact that I shot the ball most of the time). When it came to running, I only needed to look at myself and count on the work that I had done to succeed and win. I know for a fact that my experiences with cross-country and track helped to formulate my thought process when it came to hard work and my ability to succeed and lead by example.

The summer when I was going into my sixth-grade year, my dad brought my brother Elliott and me out to Southern University's football stadium and track and introduced us to the idea of running track. I really wasn't excited about the idea, because despite the fact that I'd had a little bit of success running cross-country with the junior varsity at U-High that previous year, I didn't know any of these kids. Even more, K-Y was a first-class track organization that had kids as young as seven and eight and up to eighteen who were ridiculously talented. This was where I first met Warrick Dunn, who at the time was in the midst of a great high school career locally and was just one of many unbelievable talents that K-Y had on its team. I really didn't see where I would fit in. They had sprinters, unbelievable relay teams, and great jumpers, and long distance to them was eight hundred meters. They didn't have any milers and definitely didn't have any two-milers. They looked at me as if something was wrong when I first got there and was running long distance. Even though I also started off running the eight hundred, the thought process of my new fellow track teammates seemed to be that we, as blacks in track, were supposed to be fast but not run distance—that was for the white boys. It took the entire summer, but by the end of the summer, I had won them over. Many of them would actually watch and cheer for me as I ran my races. That was a big deal, because normally people only stuck around to watch the sprints and relays.

I remember my first meet. It was at the USL (now UL-Lafayette) track, and I remember how nervous I was at the beginning of the race. My dad helped coach me, but the guy who was really my coach while I ran for K-Y was Mailen "Choo-Choo" Brooks. Coach Choo, as he's still called today, was a star athlete in his own right and had made it his main goal in life to have a positive impact on as many kids as possible. I was definitely one of those kids. I will never forget Coach Choo's voice as I ran the last curve in the eight hundred, fifteen hundred, or the three thousand meters yelling, "IT'S TIME TO GO, Collis! IT'S TIME TO GO! Where's that KICK, son?" I ended up placing second in that first race, and that was the start of a two-year summer track career for K-Y, in which I actually finished in the top fifteen in the country in both the fifteen hundred and the three thousand for my age group during that first year. The TAC National Championships were at Chapel Hill in North Carolina, and that was the first time I experienced high-level athletic competition on a national scene. That year I ran the fastest three-thousand-meter time in the state of Louisiana for an eleven-year-old, 10:41, and tied for the fastest fifteen-hundred-meter time with a time of 4:59.

As I look back on some of the journal entries that I kept from that first year, I can see the progression. Covering a couple of the journal entries from that first year of summer track may give some insight as to my thought process as I grew my competitive fire as an eleven-year-old.

June 14-15, 1991 Location: Ragin Cajun College in Lafayette [I meant UL-Lafayette], Events: 3000-11:23 (2nd Place), 1500-5:23 (2nd Place), 800-2:43 (2nd Place) Notes: "I think I did well for my first race. My goal now is to come back next week and beat Connor or lose, but not by more than ten seconds. In the 800 I did my best against Donald Ray!"

June 22, 1991 Location: Southern University in Baton Rouge, Events: 800-2:36 (2nd Place), 3000-11:30 (1st Place) Notes: "I came in second to a guy named Gino. I think I might have been able to do a little better. I didn't do very well in the 3000 because I didn't improve my time. I'll do better next week." [A note should be made to the point that I won the 3000, but because I didn't improve, I said that I didn't do very well.]

June 29-30, 1991 Location: Southern University in Baton Rouge, Events: 1500-5:16 (3rd Place), 3000-11:39 (3rd Place) Notes: "When I came in third, I came in after both Connor and Gino in both races."
July 2-6, 1991 The Athletics Congress (TAC/USA) Youth Athletics National Track and Field Championships Location: Ragin Cajun College in Lafayette, Events: 3000-10:47 (4th Place), 1500-5:16 (8th Place) Notes: "I beat Connor! I've made my

goal. I got a large medal. In the 1500 it was a large heat. There were 18! I was 8th. At the beginning I got boxed in and couldn't get out. Gino didn't run in these championships. I beat his best record and Connor's! I am the best 3000 meters runner in my age group in Louisiana."

July 12-14, 1991 Qualifying meet for the Junior Olympics in Chapel Hill, North Carolina Location: Tennessee State College, Events: 3000-11:08 (3rd Place), 1500-5:20 (3rd Place) Notes: "In the 3000 I came in third to Conner and Gino. The reason this happened was because I didn't get out fast enough. In the 1500 I came in third to the same two. I think I did my best."

July 23-28, 1991 JUNIOR OLYMPICS Location: University of North Carolina at Chapel Hill, Events: 3000-10:41 (2nd Place in my heat and 13th Place overall), 1500-4:59 (4th Place in my heat by milliseconds, and 10th Place overall) Notes: "Even though I didn't get a medal, I still did well because I beat both Gino and Conner in the 3000 and Gino beat me by 3 milliseconds in the 1500 because he stuck out his hands! That meet ended the '91' season."

Running summer track played an extremely important role in helping me develop my confidence. When I qualified with such a high finish nationally, I realized that I was one of the best in the country at something. That stoked the fire in me that I could compete and be one of the best in whatever I set out to do. I remember thinking to myself, "I could run in the Olympics, if I'm placing this high and I just started doing this. I could be one of the best in the world!" Twenty years later I still think about Coach Choo when I'm running and am nearing the end of the run. I think, "Collis, IT'S TIME TO GO!" I know that I stretch out a little bit more and run a little bit faster than if he weren't pushing me in my mind. It's amazing the types of things that stay with you.

EXTRACURRICULAR INVOLVEMENT

It wasn't just athletics that built up my competitive spirit and leadership abilities. Academics and other extracurricular activities helped play a role in my development as well. It may seem obvious that based on his and his lineage's enormous focus on academics that my dad stayed on me from an academic standpoint, and he did, but my mom was really the driving force that made sure I remained focused on keeping my grades up and competing in the classroom, as well as EVERY other area of my life. Mom would always make sure that she kept everything else outside of sports on my mind and that I was more well-rounded as a person. The idea of "How you do ANYTHING is how you do EVERYTHING" was the mind-set that I adopted from my mom, although she never stated it in those specific terms. As I mentioned earlier, she never missed a game and was as supportive as a mother could have been, but she totally embraced the role as the one who would take on the challenge of keeping me as balanced in other areas as possible. Whether it was getting me involved with the student council and school politics or trying to get me to take pride in other extracurricular activities, such as piano lessons, playing the trombone in the band, or just simply enjoying growing up and taking advantage of opportunities to participate with other kids my own age, she insisted that I stay involved. A great example was my brother's and my involvement in Jack and Jill of America. Jack and Jill of America, Inc. is a program, implemented by African American mothers in the late 1930s, to help promote healthy relationships as well as opportunities to learn and grow along with other like-minded African American children and families. I was not a huge fan of going to the Jack and Jill events, but as I look back now, I see the great deal of value those interactions had in my life.

I was extremely involved in middle school politics at University Lab School. My mom was a driving force in that participation, as she was constantly pushing me and encouraging me to run and stay involved. Both Mom and Dad would make clear that they believed that I was more than capable of running for the different offices and worthy of winning. During middle school, I was voted vice president of the middle school in the seventh grade and president while in the eighth grade. Going to a school that was probably 85 to 90 percent white, I had been programmed that my race shouldn't stop me from running and expecting to win. I remember how involved and engaged I was with running for office. Doing this in middle school started putting in my mind at an early age the possibility that I might want to become a politician as an adult.

When thinking back over what my parents—my dad, in particular—did early on to build me into the competitor I am today, I shake my head and smile. It was as if he just completely brainwashed me, in a positive way, to become some type of machine when it came to my mind-set and thought process around competing and my ability and obligation to lead. Since as far back as I can remember, my belief was that something wasn't really worth doing if there wasn't a winner and a loser. I believed that losing was unacceptable if I did not make a worthwhile attempt at competing to win. I learned that the only time not winning was OK was when I gave it my all and was just outperformed because the person was simply better than me, at that time, in that particular field. There have been very few times in my life in any area where I was just beaten to a pulp, and based on that reality, I garnered the belief that I could put myself in positions to win and lead through sheer will and work ethic. The lessons I learned from a competing and leading perspective are lessons that have stayed with me for my entire life and have made all the difference in the world.

WSTM LESSONS LEARNED

1. There are no "born leaders." Just like anything else, a person can learn and be taught how to compete and lead. It doesn't have anything to do with a person's particular athletic prowess—whether it exists or not. Putting people in positions where they'll be tested and forced to grow as a leaders, competitors, and learners is the true determining factor.

2. If you have children, give them the opportunities to succeed based on their strengths. That doesn't mean discouraging them from doing other things, but building their confidence by placing them in situations where they can display their talents—whatever they may be.

3. Understand the value of earning success despite obstacles and distractions.

4. Control your emotions under all circumstances.

5. Do all you can to be the best you can in all you do!

Chapter 4

LEARNING TO DEAL WITH THE DOUBTERS

*The person who overcomes others is
strong, but the person who
overcomes him- or herself is much
stronger. —Collis Temple III*

I was extremely fortunate to have exceptional parents who were consistently positive and extremely supportive of the activities I chose to take part in while I was growing up. They were constantly giving their evenhanded advice in helping me make decisions and helping me understand the importance of each decision that I made, as well as the possible consequences. Their unwavering support and warnings in reference to listening to those around me who may not have been as optimistic about my success were extraordinary in preparing me for handling those types of people throughout my life. Understanding the value that doubters, naysayers, and what I affectionately call "haters" brought to my life was something that I learned at an early age. Whereas many parents may attempt to shield their children from situations where they may be challenged, my parents obviously didn't put me directly in those situations, but once they arose, they would use them as the perfect opportunities to teach life lessons that would add value to me as an adult. My father is definitely a student of the Socratic method of teaching, which is based on asking questions and challenging your answers in order to force you to think.

In addition to the lessons learned from simply talking to my parents, seeing them interact with these types of circumstances in their own lives also helped to paint a vivid picture of how haters, as well as challenging and difficult situations, were to be dealt with and handled. All of that training, coupled with my many experiences and "real-life" education in dealing with negative and nonsupportive people, has put me in a position to be impermeable to the critical attacks that far too often—and, unfortunately, for most—cause others to fold up like a cheap tent in a rainstorm and quit at the first sight of negativity. I learned to use the negative people in different areas of my life as motivation and fuel to achieve more and reach even higher levels of excellence and success.

There have been far too many separate instances that resulted in my real-life education, in reference to dealing with haters, for me to go into detail about them all during this chapter of the book. I do, however, believe that using a few as examples will serve a great purpose in painting a picture of how a person can turn someone's assumed negative energy into positive fuel, which leads to greatness. Let me first preface this by saying that I totally believe that positive energy is and will always be a better motivator than negative energy, but the reality is that sometimes there are more people present who would rather NOT see you succeed than see you succeed. That being the case, learning to shift negative energy to positive fuel is a necessity to the person who plans on experiencing any level of significant success in his or her life. Fortunately for me, this was a lesson that I learned early on.

The first example that I can remember was actually in kindergarten, believe it or not. My dad always had a way of seeing things in the future and making decisions in the present moment that would have a positive impact down the road. One such decision that he and my mom made was to hold me back a year in kindergarten. The particular occurrence I want to highlight was actually during my second year in kindergarten, and the reason I remember that vividly was because two of my best friends, Geno Brown and Kyle Pourciau, had moved on to first grade, making an already small number of black kids in the class even smaller. I was the only black in my class. My teacher's name was Mrs. Pippin. Now, there's no doubt that I was an active kid, and I could sense, even at six years old, that Mrs. Pippin really didn't care for me very much. It was not until later that I learned how she had reported to the school, which subsequently reported to my parents, that I needed to get checked for mental disorders and that I would have a hard time succeeding in a normal classroom environment. The way I have been told that the story goes was that my mother was made aware by the school of Mrs. Pippin's opinions and was extremely bothered by them. She told my father, and he said something to the effect of, "There's nothing wrong with that boy! That woman is crazy—we're not getting him checked; we're taking him out of there!" My parents have never been the type of parents who sided with their children even when their children were in the wrong. Right was right and wrong was wrong, and it was that simple. If anything, they worked very well with my teachers in helping my brothers and me accomplish our goals, but they realized that this woman was just wrong, and they would never just sit back and deal with that, especially not my mom. To make a long story short, I ended up leaving Runnels the following year and going to University Laboratory School, where I remained all the way through the twelfth grade. I excelled at U-High, and in the sixth grade when I was named Outstanding Boy for the year, was voted president of my sixth-grade class, and had a 4.0 GPA, I actually came up with the idea to copy the awards, put them in a folder, and send them to Mrs. Pippin with a short note thanking her for the motivation.

From a sports perspective, I vividly remember standing near the doorway of the gym and the lobby of the Sports Academy, holding my basketball and watching a House League game, while my dad, Lester Roberts, and a couple of other men talked behind me, not knowing I was listening—or maybe my dad did know I was listening. Nevertheless, the conversation was relatively simple; my dad was explaining to them why I would have a shot at playing major college basketball, and, based on their responses, they thought that that was a hilarious suggestion. The men were saying, "There's no way, Collis—he's too slow; he's clumsy, always falling down; he's too weak and scrawny..." and so on. Now, they were saying it in a joking way, because they wouldn't totally just laugh at me outright because of my dad's clout, but I knew they were serious. I always took that kind of stuff personally, and I don't know how healthy it was, but I somehow internalized it and used it as fuel at an early age. Today, if you walk into the Sports Academy, there's a huge signed poster of a great game photo of me taking off to dunk the ball in my LSU uniform; it's only about three feet from where one of the men laughed at my father as he talked about the athletic success that his son would one day experience.

My dad got me running cross-country on University's junior varsity when I was in the fifth grade. By the seventh grade, I was vying for the top spot on the varsity team. I remember the conversations with upperclassmen on my own team trying to mentally outwit me and belittle me in attempts to get in my head. My cross-country experiences really helped to build my character as a young man and as an athlete. In other sports I was competing in my grade level, but I was forced to deal with a different set of circumstances once I started competing against older boys who weren't very excited about not only being beat, but sometimes being embarrassed by someone younger than them in a sport that, at our school, no one black had really ever been competitive in. I learned to deal with a different set of doubters from my cross-country experiences. These were the smart, deceptive, and subtle doubters who weren't as obvious, but seemed to be worse because you weren't exactly sure, unless you were aware, of where they were coming from. I remember instances where the guys would make blanketing racial comments like, "We didn't think that black guys could do anything but sprint, Collis." As I would run, I would think of the things that were said and the snide remarks and use them to press on through the pain and push myself to run harder and faster in attempts to beat them as badly as I could. There were very few times when I'd confront those upperclassmen verbally; I remember being in the seventh and eighth grades and thinking, "I don't have to say much—I'm saying enough by beating them so badly when we run."

The experiences in dealing with the doubters in terms of my sports career were numerous. In later chapters, I'll take the opportunity to go into further detail about some of those experiences and how they helped shape my mentality in dealing with those types of people. There is one instance that I would like to bring out at this point, and that was the experience of my first trip to the Dixie Basketball Camp in Mississippi, run by then-LSU athletic director Joe Dean. It was a two-session overnight camp that was held for two weeks at a time during the summer. I was nine years old, and the youngest campers other than me were twelve. I was also the only black camper, as I remember it, in a camp of about 150 campers. I remember calling my dad and asking him to come pick me up, begging him to take me out of my misery. The camp was only six days long, but after two and a half days, I felt that I was totally out of place. The only place I felt any comfort was when we were on the floor playing, and those moments didn't seem often enough. After the third day of camp, my dad came and picked me up, and we made the short thirty-minute drive to his hometown of Kentwood, Louisiana. We walked inside my grandparents' home, where they still had a shrine of their children's achievements along the wall of the main hallway of the house. Many of my father's accomplishments were neatly framed and displayed on the wall. This was without a doubt the work of my grandmother. I remember the feeling of pride I'd get every time I went to my grandparents' home and looked at the pictures of all of my aunts and all the things they'd accomplished, and specifically the things my father had done. This particular time I walked down the hall, looking up at the articles and pictures and thinking about how I couldn't wait to be featured in articles like that. My dad was slightly trailing me, and he said, "If you don't go back, you can't play basketball anymore. We don't EVER quit what we start, especially because of the things that other people may say or think that cause us to be uncomfortable." The second part wasn't even necessary; there was no way that I was going to allow what I believed to be a blossoming and promising basketball career to be ended at nine years old because of some people who doubted my ability due to my youth and because I was the only one of my ethnic background to stick it out at a week-long basketball camp in Mississippi. As I've thought back about the conversation that summer evening, I think that my dad may have called out the big guns to get me to stick it out at the camp, threatening my future career as a basketball player—something he knew I loved—but I've always been glad he did it because I felt so good at the end of the week when I had completed camp and was recognized as the youngest camper there. When I went back to the camp two years later with my best friend Geno Brown, we had an unbelievable time, and I felt like a veteran.

That Dixie Basketball Camp incident was a huge event in my life because from that point on, I never started a season in any sport, or started anything else, for that matter, and thought that quitting during the middle of it was okay under any circumstances. No matter the situation, I had the mentality that if I started something, I would decide whether I wanted to continue or not at the season's end. That also went for my academic career, explaining why I never dropped a college course. NOT QUITTING, NO MATTER WHAT, has been a major mind-set that has permeated my entire life, and as you'd expect, it's made a huge difference in my life.

WSTM LESSONS LEARNED

1. Never prejudge people's ability. You don't know what they have inside them. Don't allow others who may prejudge your ability to affect your performance.
2. Make a habit of not quitting. It sounds simple enough, but it's much easier said than done. No matter how big or small of a commitment, or whom you make it to (yourself or someone else)— DON'T QUIT!

Chapter 5

LEARNING THE POWER OF GOAL SETTING

Destiny is no matter of chance. It's a matter of choice.
It's not a thing to be waited for, it's a thing to
be achieved. —William Jennings Bryan

Goal-setting works as long as you do. —Collis Temple III

When I made what at the time was the toughest decision of my life to leave basketball and pursue a career in business, I didn't realize that almost all of the same staples of success that had helped me succeed in things I had done prior to that point in my life would also apply to my success in business. It was a pleasant surprise when my primary mentor in business, Bill Whittle, echoed everything that I had learned from my own parents in terms of goal setting. He even had a more specific and definite way to go about setting goals and accomplishing the things that I was looking to achieve.

Goal setting became a powerful part of my life relatively early on because of the things that my parents taught me about life in general, as well as through my own competitive experiences in the classroom, extracurricular activities, and especially in the realm of sports. The first time I can truly remember having and setting goals was during the 1990 cross-country season when I was an eleven-year-old fifth grader. Things got even more intense that next summer during summer track with the K-Y Track Club, as I have mentioned earlier. Take a look at my focus on reaching and achieving goals that I set for myself in these entries from the journals that I kept that summer:

> June 14-15, 1991 Location: Ragin Cajun College in Lafayette [I meant UL-Lafayette], Events: 3000-11:23 (2nd Place), 1500-5:23 (2nd Place), 800-2:43 (2nd Place) Notes: "I think I did well for my first race. My goal now is to come back next week and beat Connor or lose, but not by more than ten seconds. In the 800 I did my best against Donald Ray!"

> July 2-6, 1991 The Athletics Congress (TAC/USA) Youth Athletics National Track and Field Championships Location: Ragin Cajun College in Lafayette, Events: 3000-10:47 (4th Place), 1500-5:16 (8th Place) Notes: "I beat Connor! I've made my goal. I got a large medal. In the 1500 it was a large heat. There were 18! I was 8th. At the beginning I got boxed in and couldn't get out. Gino didn't run in these championships. I beat his best record and Connor's! I am the best 3000 meters runner in my age group in Louisiana."

As you look at the entries, you can see that I had a strong focus on hitting certain targets and reaching specific points. I realized early on while running cross-country and track that I was running against myself and the clock, and although I was obviously striving to beat the two other boys who at the time were considered two of the best distance runners in my age group in the state, I was still focused on doing the best I could first and foremost. I still smile when I read these entries because the idea and concept of setting goals and competing is so foreign to many people, and as I read I truly realize how I've been programmed from such an early age and how I perpetuated that programming in myself as I continued to grow as a person.

One of the many things that came from this experience that I still use extensively today (and that quite possibly made the writing of this book that much easier) was the idea from my dad to literally write notes, or journal, after every cross-country meet. I would write my feelings about the race, about how I ran, about the course, and whatever else I thought about. (He also made the suggestion for me to do this in terms of my basketball games, but I didn't do nearly as good of a job with basketball, except for my sophomore and junior seasons of high school.) I started journaling for everything after this: my feelings after awards banquets, basketball camps, and almost everything else I did. I also credit the concept of journaling with helping to make me a lot more comfortable with putting my thoughts down on paper. Journaling helped me a year later when my dad introduced the idea of writing my goals down as well, a concept that has had a major impact on my entire life.

I learned the power of short-term and long-term goal setting from many different experiences. In the sixth grade, my dad got me to write down my goals on a piece of loose-leaf paper, put a piece of tape on the back, and tape them to my mirror, where I would see them every morning, recite them, and think about accomplishing them. Another noteworthy occurrence that took place that year happened in my art class. The art teacher asked us to write out our first names and to also describe several things about ourselves by drawing within the letters of our names. What I drew in *COLLIS* was a basketball, me shooting a jump shot, a scoreboard showing my team winning the game, me spinning the ball on my finger, me dribbling, and me in a Louisiana State University (LSU) uniform with the number my father had worn, forty-one.

That was exactly what happened: I went to LSU, shot—and made—a lot of jump shots, and won many games, and the entire time, I was wearing number forty-one!

LSU became a part of my goal setting early on because of my involvement with the program. Ironically enough, in a move that would prove to be prophetic foreshadowing, long-time LSU coach Dale Brown gave my dad a letter of intent for me to attend LSU on a basketball scholarship at the hospital on the day I was born! I guess I was always destined to play at LSU! The current LSU coach, Johnny Jones, also sent a letter of intent to my son, Collis IV, jumping through all the hoops the NCAA and LSU compliance department had him jump through in the process! I started my LSU career as a ball boy with the team in the third grade. I took my job really seriously, and I got a chance to be around some of the greatest players in LSU history, guys like Chris Jackson (now named Mahmoud Abdul-Rauf) and Shaquille O'Neal. It was such a great experience to see those guys blossoming as young men and excelling in such a major way on the national scene. I remember thinking, "I KNOW these guys. They are STARS, and I get a chance to talk to them and deal with them on a weekly basis! I could experience the same success that they're having!" Thinking back now and realizing that I was only in the third grade, it's funny, but I really remember having those thoughts that I wanted to make people feel the way they made me feel when I watched them, especially Mahmoud. He was ridiculously amazing! Out of all the exploits of Mahmoud Abdul-Rauf—averaging over thirty points as a freshman in the SEC; scoring fifty-five points in his first SEC game against Florida on national television; returning for his sophomore campaign; and, with a stacked team that had four first-round draft picks, still averaging 27.5 points a game—out of all of the great moves, "wow!" moments, bottom-of-the-net threes, there was one thing that I witnessed that made the biggest impact on me. My dad and I were leaving an LSU football game. (For those who don't know, football at LSU and in southern Louisiana for many is almost a religious experience. Although we enjoyed it, it never was like that for us.) We were leaving the game after the third quarter to beat the traffic, and I don't remember if LSU was winning or losing the game; it really isn't relevant to this story. As Dad and I walked away from Death Valley toward my dad's truck, which was probably almost a mile to a half mile away, we walked by the Pete Maravich Assembly Center (PMAC). The bottom part of the facility at the time was called "the Dungeon" because of its location under the gym. This is where pickup games were played and where many practices took place. It was probably about 9:30 p.m. on a Saturday night; LSU was playing a football game, and we heard a basketball bouncing in the Dungeon. Dad looked at me, and he already knew what I wanted to do—find out who was in there, of course. We walked down the steps, opened the door to the Dungeon, and there, going as hard as if he were playing Tennessee on national television, was Mahmoud Abdul-Rauf. He was soaked, and, amazingly, when watching him practice by himself, I got the same chills as when I watched him hit back-to-back-to-back threes in high-stakes games over and over again. His focus, his intensity, and his passion were evident and contagious. I wanted to be like that. I wanted to feel like that about basketball and make others feel like that about me playing. That first year during his freshman year, he was featured on the cover of *Sports Illustrated*. When I saw that, I remember believing that I too could become a phenomenal basketball player and a pro, if I set goals and worked like I had seen him working. Watching Mahmoud working as he was that night when nobody was watching was huge for me; it helped to cement some of the things that I had already been taught by my parents. I equated hard work with goal setting and goal accomplishment. It became a mentality that was burned into my brain.

I remember setting goals in a progression during my middle school years in relation to my involvement in student government. I set goals during the sixth grade to be the sixth-grade class president, but I also set goals that year that progressed to, two years later, to become president of the entire middle school as an eighth grader. Those were big goals that meant a great deal to me. During my middle school years, I didn't lose an election. The consistent success in student government bolstered my already robust self-esteem and self-confidence, as well as my belief that goal setting worked as long as I did! During my middle school years, I also earned and enjoyed a grade point average that floated between 3.57 and 4.0 for my entire time in middle school. That was important to me because although I never thought of myself as the smartest kid in my class, I did think of myself as one of the smartest. I knew that I would outwork everybody, and I learned that setting goals to perform at a high level in every area was not only what I should do, but something that I wanted to do. I started to formulate a thought process that had me believing that in any area in which I wanted to excel, GOAL SETTING coupled with HARD WORK would get DONE whatever I wanted to get done.

Once I made it to high school, I had cemented in my brain that I could in fact accomplish whatever I wanted. As a high school freshman, I once again put my goal-setting premise to the test and set goals before my first high school campaign to make the varsity team that first year and to become an all-district performer as a sophomore, an all-state performer as a junior, and an All-American as a senior. My goal was to culminate my high school career with a college scholarship to a major Division I university (preferably LSU). My desire to earn a spot on the varsity basketball team at University High School as a freshman, despite the normal custom being that freshmen didn't play on the varsity team, was not an accomplishment that was immune to my belief in my ability to succeed. Despite being a five-foot-seven, 120-pound freshman with big feet who was clumsy and not the quickest, I earned a spot on the varsity team that first year, even having a major breakout game the first game of the year and scoring twenty-two points! It was just further confirmation for me that goal setting worked. As a freshman I averaged slightly less than six points and two assists a game on the varsity squad and started every game for the junior varsity team. Going into my sophomore year, I was looking forward to a great year. Check out the entry at the beginning of the journal I kept prior to the season:

"Well, here I am a sophomore. Last year I played well for a freshman. I have big expectations for this year and hope that I play better. After lifting weights over the summer and gaining twenty pounds (120-140), I'm ready to 'show my stuff.'"

Here was my entry at the end of the year:

"Year in Review: Well, it was a pretty good year. I was voted as a first-team All-District selection by the coaches in the district. U-High posted its first winning season under Roy Hill (16-11), and I was chosen, by the coach, to be the best offensive player. For both honors I received a plaque. I think next year we should win state. No playoff bid this year."

That sophomore year I averaged 16.1 points, 5.1 assists, and 2.3 rebounds a game. I started for most of the year, and, as you read, I accomplished my goal of being named to the all-district team. What has not yet been mentioned is the fact that during that second year of high school, I had grown three more inches, and by the year's end was five feet ten inches tall. By no means was I an impressive physical specimen, nor was I a towering presence in stature, but my growth as a player and a person continued, and it was powered to a large extent by the goals that I had set before my freshman season.

Goal setting was and is a central point of importance in my life and a major reason for the modest success I've been able to achieve so far. I am continually striving to set goals and live up to those goals and expectations I have of myself every day. There have only been a few times that I have accomplished a goal that I set on time in the business world, but setting them and legitimately striving to hit them has been what my career thus far in business has been all about. I also have learned that once I get close to achieving a set goal, I should throw it out a little bit further and see if I can accomplish it at an even higher level in a shorter period of time.

WSTM LESSONS LEARNED

1. Ask yourself, "What type of connection do I have with goal setting and work ethic? Do I have a negative mentality, a positive
mentality, or no mentality at all based on past programming?" If
the answer to that question isn't a favorable one, fix it quickly.
2. Make sure you are setting goals based on your own effort instead
of basing your goals on what others around you are doing or accomplishing. Set goals that are "stretchingly realistic" for YOU!

Chapter 6

TRAVELING: EXPANDING MY WORLDVIEW

We travel not to escape life, but for life
not to escape us. —Anonymous

I have been extremely blessed throughout my life to have been afforded the opportunities to travel to several places around the world throughout North and South America, Europe, and Africa. These opportunities presented themselves early on in my life entirely due to my parents' hard work, diligence, and success in building a phenomenal business that legitimately gave them opportunities where they could take my brothers and me on the type of trips and vacations that the person of average financial means could not take. My belief is that my opportunity to travel all over the United States and abroad widened my worldview and expanded my frame of reference, giving me a larger pool of experiences to draw ideas from. I am a firm believer that my paternal grandparents, Collis and Shirley, and their mentality also had a great influence on my travel experiences due to the way they raised their children and the subsequent construction of my father's mentality as it related to what true travel and exposure were about. My father's mind-set was that we should see as much as we could, go as many places as we could, and be exposed to as much as possible. It is also a great credit to my mother, who, although she was not as well traveled as my father, totally bought into his mind-set and supported him in exposing us to as much as they possibly could.

The first time I can actually remember getting on an airplane was when I was in the first grade. The reason I say *actually remember* is because my daughter Monet, before her second birthday, had already flown over ten different times to places like Puerto Rico, Orlando, Las Vegas, New York, and the like. My son Collis had already been to Disney World and the New York Stock Exchange within a week before he turned six weeks old. I may have flown before I was in the first grade, but that is the first I can remember. It was a Friday, and our parents picked my brothers and me up with the suitcases in the backseat packed and ready. I was so excited! I remember saying as we rode to the airport, "Mama, we're gonna fly in a plane!" That first flight took us to Disney—I don't remember if it was Disney World or Disneyland, but I remember that it was Disney.

My parents took us on family trips that were in line with the track season during the years we ran summer track. We got to go see Carlsbad Caverns National Park, which is located in New Mexico. It was amazing to have the chance to witness the unbelievable beauty of the underground caves. We also had the opportunity to visit the Grand Canyon National Park in Arizona twice. The first time we visited the canyons, we actually walked down what is considered to be one of the Eight Wonders of the world. These were experiences that I quickly realized that many of my friends were not being exposed to. That realization came from the looks on many of their faces on my return and in my attempts to explain our travels. Most of my friends would almost look at me as if to say, "Why would walking underground even be fun?" or "What's so great about going to see a bunch of rocks?" Unfortunately, they just didn't understand, which makes it all the more sad, because if they did not see the value in exposure then, unless they come in contact with some type of life-changing experience, they will not be in a position to ever be able to expose their own children.

Some of the most fun that I've had traveling came on the several family snow-skiing trips that we took. Still to this day, snow skiing is one of the most fun activities that I've experienced. We went snow skiing in Oregon, Colorado several times, and New Mexico. I have since snow skied in Canada also. I know the thought: "Black people snow skiing?" You can imagine that I know the look even better, having had to deal with it EVERY TIME we got back from one of our snow-skiing escapades.

The three trips that I valued the most growing up were the family vacation we took to Ghana and the entire west coast of Africa when I was in the sixth grade; just me and my dad going to the Million Man March in Washington, DC, when I was a high school sophomore; and me and my brothers and my father going to Egypt before my senior year in high school. All three of these trips were unbelievable, and we had a great time! With my two trips to the African continent, the question was always the same: "Why did you go there?" That was always very annoying, because somehow I knew that had I said I had traveled to France or Spain, the response and question would have been totally different. My response was always a quick, "Because we were on vacation, and I wanted to see where my ancestors came from. Wouldn't you?"

When we went to Ghana, we started off in the capital city of Accra and stayed in the University of Ghana's student housing. It was an extremely interesting experience. Traveling abroad did give me a much greater appreciation for all the luxuries and blessings that I experienced in my everyday life, things as small as having choices when it came to what was available to eat, and having more than enough. No matter where I went, I always managed to find a basketball court, and Ghana was no different. During our first few days there on the campus, I found some outdoor courts where some older teenagers were playing ball. A few were from the United States, but most were from Ghana. One of the guys from the United States was from New York, and his parents were professors at the university. After we had conversed a few times, he said, "You must be from down South somewhere. I hear it in your voice." I told him where I was from, and asked him where he was from. I learned that day that basketball was a universal language, and although I couldn't communicate with most of the guys, we had a great time playing together. We saw some beautiful things in Ghana, but mostly it was the people, who were so warm, cordial, and inviting. From the beautiful resort that looked out over the Atlantic Ocean, to the University of Ghana campus, to the final place of many Africans before they were shipped to America, and even to Sierra Leone, where the people were not nearly as friendly and there was a much stronger French influence, the best part of the trip were the experiences and the people.

Traveling to DC for the quick, one-day turnaround that was the Million Man March with my dad was a liberating and proud feeling. I have always loved Washington, DC. First, some of my favorite family members lived there, the Tulls, and visiting them was always great, but I loved the symbolism of it being the nation's capital and the most powerful city in the world. Much of my love for DC came from the fact that my Uncle Knox, Aunt Brenda, and first cousins lived there, and I already mentioned earlier how highly I thought of them as a family. Having the chance to go the march with them was great. The Million Man March, to me, was an extremely important event that was called by the Honorable Minister Louis Farrakhan of the Nation of Islam for October 16, 1995. I was in the tenth grade, and remember the pride that I felt when I would answer the question, "So, where were you Monday, Collis?" It was almost comical the day after listening to newscasters talking about there not being one million men present that Monday in DC. The reality is that there were OVER one million men there, but even if there had not been, why would the number of people have been the focus of the conversation instead of what the meeting was called to be about—which was unity, atonement, and brotherhood among African American men? The opportunity to experience an event as powerful as the Million Man March was something that I will always cherish, and having my dad make it possible made it that much more fulfilling.

The last major vacation we took prior to me graduating from high school was a trip to Egypt that my dad and my two brothers and I went on. I was going into my senior year, and it was in the midst of the most intense recruiting time of my basketball career. My parents had been separated for about six months, which explained why it was just my brothers and father. Going to Egypt was utterly amazing. Dad had been there thirty years earlier, and getting an opportunity to see the pyramids, the Sphinx, and everything else was a breathtaking experience. Seeing how advanced the Egyptian civilization was and coming to the realization that these were people who looked just like me and were on the continent of Africa gave me a great sense of pride. Hearing the intense and immense history on the tours we took all around the country of Egypt and seeing the different things that had been done to hide or discredit the advances and true identity of the Egyptians was also extremely enlightening and informative. Another interesting point was that while we were there and the recruiting calls were coming from the various schools that were offering me scholarships, it was amusing for me to hear my aunt, Colleen, who was handling some of the calls, tell me how the coaches would respond when she let them know that I was in Egypt on vacation! I assume that most of the coaches realized that they were not recruiting that average run-of-the-mill kid who had not been exposed to a great deal. I got a kick out of that.

Having the opportunity to travel on a regular basis is something I have never taken for granted. I have always believed that the exposure helped me grow as a person and truly value what I'm blessed to have, how I'm blessed to live, and whom I'm blessed to spend time around. As much of a mind-opening experience as traveling was for me, it also helped to improve the already grateful spirit that I had as a boy and young man.

COLLIS TEMPLE III

WSTM LESSONS LEARNED

1. Make time to learn about the world around you. Expose your-
    self and your children to as many travel opportunities as you can
    within your financial means.
2. Always be grateful for what you have and how you live. Be cog-
    nizant of the lifestyles of others and develop an appreciation for
    how they live. Different doesn't necessarily mean inferior.

Chapter 7

"WHY?"–MY MILITANT STREAK

*The Confederacy's cornerstone rests upon the
great truth that the Negro is not equal to
the white man. This government is the first in
the history of the world based on this great
physical and moral truth. —Alexander H.
Stevens, vice president of the Confederacy*

*I am not a racist. I am against every form of racism
and segregation—EVERY form of discrimination.
I believe in human beings, and that all human
beings should be respected as such,
regardless of their color. —Malcolm X*

"WHAT I DON'T UNDERSTAND"-1989, Fourth Grade,
Nine Years Old
   I may be wrong about what I'm saying here, or
someone might not like it but, I know it's true. This
is what I don't understand.

I don't understand that most white children don't know about black peoples' history but, black children know all about white peoples' history. Just a few weeks ago, I came across a white high school boy. He didn't even know who Malcolm-X was, but, when I asked a black fourth grader she knew all about him!

White children are always walking around with Michael Jordan shoes on or Bo Jackson shoes on. They wear Michael Jordan shirts and pants. They know all about M.C. Hammer and Kid 'n' Play but, can't say who Malcolm-X was or who Nelson Mandela is. I asked a fifth grade white boy to tell me who Malcolm-X and Martin Luther King Jr. were. He could tell me a little bit about Martin Luther King, Jr. but, had never heard about Malcolm-X.

Now, almost all books on George Washington says he's America's father, when he had black slaves. Blacks are a part of America too. I think, that Martin Luther King, Jr. should be called "Black America's Father."

These are all things that I don't understand!

Pretty deep stuff for a fourth grader, right? Despite the grammatical mistakes, as I look back on my writing as an elementary student, I am pretty impressed by the way I processed thoughts and was able to put them down on paper. I'm even more impressed with where my mind was at nine years old. I could perceive the disconnect between what was being taught to me in school as it related to history and the fact that the many accomplishments of blacks in the United States were unseen, ignored, or many times totally unknown by not only white students but by the white teachers who were teaching me and who were to be considered experts in terms of the subject matter as well. That was where my mind-set was then, and it is not very far from there now, although I've grown a great deal to be able to understand some of the things I had questions about back then. Those ideas and concepts were the things that I was focusing on and thinking about every day as a nine- and ten-year-old. My parents did a phenomenal job of keeping me grounded and FULLY aware of who I was, what I was, and why I should be proud of all of it.

The third, fourth, and fifth grades made up what I consider to be an extremely important time in my life when I experienced a true social awakening as it related to race relations and politics in the United States, in Louisiana, in my own life, and with my family. While I was in the third grade, I remember my experience with the first presidential election that I can remember caring about the outcome of; it was in 1988 between Michael Dukakis, a Democrat, and George H. Bush, a Republican. I can remember the conversations with classmates, and George Bush actually came to Baton Rouge and spoke at the Pete Maravich Assembly Center on LSU's campus during the campaign. Our class took a field trip and went to the event. I felt so out of place because I knew my parents were voting for Michael Dukakis. Listening to the comments that not only my classmates but also the adults who were around me were making was extremely interesting and insightful even at that young age. This was my first true understanding about national politics and race in the United States. I remember learning that, for the most part, blacks voted Democrat and tended to be more liberal in terms of their political viewpoints. My early understanding was that Democrats were, in many cases, in favor of more programs where the government was involved to a greater extent. I learned that the programs that my parents ran for foster kids, juvenile delinquent children, mentally retarded adults, and chemically dependent people were funded by both the federal and state governments. I saw voting Democrat as keeping my parents in business, as well as the more than three hundred employees they had, and also as helping the people whom they were serving, who in many cases would have ended up homeless or in jail unjustly due to circumstances they truly didn't have total control over. I remember learning that I didn't always need to look at just my personal situation in terms of making political decisions and choices about the ways that I voted, but to also make decisions based on how it could affect others as well.

Being raised by extremely conscious parents helped me to always remain clear about the pride I should have as an African American and also the struggles that those who came before me dealt with in order for me to be able to enjoy the things that I enjoyed. I believe that I had two of the best examples of how to show black pride without being overbearing and confrontational in watching my parents. The movies *Roots*, *Glory*, *Malcolm X*, and *Boyz in the Hood* were some of my favorites that helped me better understand the realities of life during this time in my life.

There were many mornings as we cooked and ate breakfast that my dad would turn on the television to the always-controversial ultra-conservative Rush Limbaugh show. You may be totally surprised that a completely aware black man would expose his children to someone like Limbaugh, but you also don't know my dad. He told me, "Collis, you always have to know how the other side is thinking and what they're saying and doing so you can stay several steps ahead." That assertion, made while I was still in elementary school, always stuck with me!

When I first saw Alex Haley's entire *Roots* saga, I remember feeling everything from pride to extreme anger. I loved watching the entire process that took Haley's family from the west coast of Africa to his subsequent return and enlightenment about his ancestry. I remember an English project I had in middle school where my teacher asked us to write about our ancestry. I asked a questions of my parents and aunts and went back as far as I could (this was before ancestry.com existed) before having to make up a little bit, showing my family's roots back to the Watusi tribe in West Africa. I did research on and picked that tribe because they were known as a tall people, and with my father being six foot eight, I figured that it was a justifiable choice. I really believed I had done a great job of writing the paper, but was extremely disappointed when I got the paper back and received a C−; the teacher said that my assumptions were unrealistic. I remember thinking, "How do you expect me to know exactly where my family originated from, considering the brutal and inhumane circumstances of American slavery?" I had classmates who were writing with precise clarity and sureness about their families' beginnings in places all over Europe; that's when I realized that I didn't know for sure and was unsure if I would ever know. It was almost a demeaning feeling, which was made worse by the reminder that my rendition of *Roots* in my family was fact only to a point, and then it became a fairy tale that I could only HOPE was true to a certain extent.

The things that we remember are sometimes strange, but the strong feelings that we feel usually help us to remember things better. That was definitely the case when my mom brought my brother and me to see the movie *Glory*. I remember watching the movie in the theater and being so mad and frustrated. From Matthew Broderick's character, the young lieutenant, to Morgan Freeman's character and especially to Denzel Washington's character, all of them left an impression. The scene that had me the most heated was when Denzel's character was whipped for leaving and looking for some shoes. The look on my face as he was being whipped was without a doubt a mirror image of the look on his, as I teared up and had a reaction of total disgust and frustration. I remember walking out of the movie thinking, "Why would I want to go the armed forces and represent a country that treated its soldiers that way?"

When I watched Denzel Washington and Spike Lee's portrayal of Malcolm X in the movie titled with the same name, it instantly became my favorite movie. Lee no doubt took some cinematic liberty with small parts of the movie, but it was closely related to Alex Haley's autobiography of Malcolm X. I felt similar feelings watching this movie as I had with others I had seen that dealt with race in the United States. In my opinion, the consciousness of the United States of America tries to suppress or distort the memory and legacy of Malcolm X to a great extent. The feedback that I get even today from people ignorant of the facts is that he was a racist and bigot. There may have been a time during his life while under the tutelage of Elijah Muhammed and the Nation of Islam when that was the case, but I don't believe that he ever preached hate.

In my evaluation, his teaching revolved totally around self-reliance and empowerment. It revolved around raising your self-esteem and defending yourself and family "by any means necessary." It's funny, because under circumstances involving foreign relationships, the powers that be in the United States have always had the mentality that we will defend this country by any means necessary, but when an extremely assertive, aggressive, outspoken and articulate, intelligent, self-educated, well-dressed black man spoke the same words in reference to black people in the United States, he was seen as totally out of line and as a HUGE threat, a demagogue. He was labeled a total radical and, although on a different end of the spectrum, was thought of as being on par with the Ku Klux Klan. It was always confusing to me, even at young age, that with all the gruesomely extreme and horrible things that the Ku Klux Klan and groups like it had done to black people, someone who simply spoke out against them and anyone else who thought similarly would be considered anything but sane. The Nation of Islam never had a history of hanging, shooting, beating, and raping white people. Malcolm X simply preached that people should defend themselves. I think about my mentor in business, Bill Whittle, who happens to be white, saying that his father always told him, "You better never start a fight, but if someone starts one with you, you better not run from it, or I'll whip your butt when you get home." In my estimation, all Malcolm X was ever saying, even in his days with the Nation, was that he would defend himself and his family at all costs. When he left the Nation of Islam, his broad and wide-spreading indictment that ALL white people were horrible was softened to a great extent based on his own experiences on his hajj to Mecca.

Thinking about Malcolm X's famous speech when he said, "We declare our right on this earth to be a man, to be a human being, to be given the rights of a human being, to be respected as a human being, in this society, on this earth, in this day, which we intend to bring into existence by any means necessary," who would not want those same rights, and be ready to take the same action to achieve them?

The first time I heard Louis Farrakhan speak at Southern University, I was in the sixth grade, and it was such an eye-opening experience. His ability to speak and break down his points in a simple and concise way made it easy for me, even as a twelve-year-old, to understand exactly what he was saying and the meanings associated with it. I remember loving his ability to articulate many of the things that I was feeling at the time. I have always admired Louis Farrakhan as an orator and truth teller.

I dealt with racism in my own way while growing up. I truly can't imagine how my father, being one of only a handful of African American students on campus, had to feel dealing with it in the early 1970s on LSU's campus, and how my grandfather must have felt while watching him deal with it and guiding him through that maze. However, I have had my own share of instances that helped formulate my mentality in reference to race relations—my own experiences in dealing with overt and covert racism and how I felt about these experiences. Several of my experiences came from athletic situations that I dealt with in middle school and high school. The first example of overt racism in my own life from an athletics perspective was at the awards banquet for University High in 1993. I remember that despite the fact that I was only an eighth grader, I had won the most races on the varsity cross-country team and had run the fastest time on the team during the state meet. I remember walking into the banquet excited about the awards I knew I was sure to win. Nothing like I was expecting to happen actually happened. I didn't get any awards other than the normal letterman award. In addition to what I saw as a gross oversight, I watched as the same thing happened to the African Americans on the football team. These were obvious and, to me, extremely frustrating examples of young men whose accomplishments were simply ignored by their all-white coaches. For instance, there was a tenth-grade running back who had a thousand-yard year and 3.2 GPA who received no awards that night, other than the awards that were voted on by those who were not dependent on the coach turning their names in for consideration. Other much less talented individuals who hadn't contributed nearly as much received award after award. It could be said that this is an unfair example, with me being on the outside looking in, being that I wasn't on the football team, but the reality is that I knew all of the guys involved, and the young black men weren't head cases in the least. It was just a set of unfortunate examples of remnants of what still existed in the minds of many people in the United States. The conversations with my parents, and specifically my father, were intense and lasting after sessions like the one at the banquet. The things I learned about how to deal with those circumstances are things that I still hold dear today.

The few times I've been called a "nigger" by someone white have led to vivid memories, because it wasn't something that happened with regularity while growing up during the 1990s, but the fact that there were those who still felt comfortable enough to say it to my face got under my skin. There was never a doubt in my mind that it was said often behind my back, but the few times it was said to my face led to physical confrontations that never ended well for the person who felt compelled to call me out of my name. One of my most vivid remembrances occurred during civics while I was in the tenth grade. I was about to go to the Million Man March in DC, when somehow the subject was turned by one of my classmates to what you call an ignorant white person. His smart-aleck answer was a "wigger," and then he looked at me and said, smiling, "But Collis is black, so we can just call him a nigger!" I will admit that the kid who said it was easily the most socially awkward of anyone in my class, but he was intelligent and far from mentally challenged. Somehow that day, he had temporarily lost his mind. I remember "clicking" for a brief second and not thinking about the consequences, and before I knew it, despite the fact that we were still sitting in our desks, I had full-out punched him dead in the right side of his face—full contact, directly on his cheek bone. Fortunately for me, we were in civics class, and that teacher happened to be one of my favorites. Not only did I not get in trouble, but he sent the young man to the principal's office and told him that he had no business calling me that and had gotten exactly what he should have, and that he was lucky it wasn't worse.

My mentality on how to deal with race relations was molded to a large extent by one of the best I've seen do it, my dad. He has a great ability to force people to focus on him as a man first and a black man second. He also has a clear understanding of the mind-set and mentality of many of those around him and what will be necessary for him to achieve his goals and the goals of whatever group of people he is looking to help accomplish something of significance. In looking back on how he built the foundation of my maturity in relation to dealing with race, I learned that my parents were geniuses in exposing me early on to all types of people, and primarily to the majority race in the United States. My parents' exposure early on afforded me the opportunity to truly learn and understand how to act and react when situations arose later in my life. "The cream will always rise to the top, Collis. No matter what the situation, everything will work itself out." When I got overly frustrated and worked up about race situations, and other circumstances in general, that is what my dad would tell me, and he was always right.

WSTM LESSONS LEARNED

1. When it comes to politics and race, many have very strong opinions. Make sure to do your best to listen to both sides and make a determination as to which side you like based on factual and solid information, as well as personal experience.
2. Expose yourself and your children to as many types of people as possible. Learning to coexist with different people will go a long way toward your success in life.

Chapter 8

"I DESERVE TO WIN": MY LAST TWO YEARS OF HIGH SCHOOL

Every day I'm HUSTLIN'... —Rick Ross

U-HIGH BASKETBALL PREVIEW 1996-97, JUNIOR YEAR: This may be my most important season. I finally got my first letter, but it's from a small school. This is the year, but the football team is doing well, so there may be trouble before they come back. We aren't very deep.

This was the entry leading into my junior year; notice I realized the importance of the season in the ultimate accomplishment of my overall high school goal, earning a major Division I scholarship. This was a pivotal year for me. As I look back and read what I said during that entry, "This may be my most important season" and "this is the year," I see that I clearly knew what was at stake and made a decision early on that if I was going to accomplish my goal, I was going to have to work harder than I ever had. I did, waking up every morning that year between 4:45 a.m. and 5:15 a.m. and working out with weights, plyometric programs (explosiveness drills), and shooting and dribbling drills. By year's end, I had grown three more inches, was six foot one, and had gained twenty more pounds, weighing in at about 160. That year, in alignment with my goals, I was named co-MVP of the district, all-district first team, all-metro, and all-state second team with averages of twenty-three points, 5.2 assists, and 4.5 rebounds. I legitimately earned the respect of several of my peers that year, but most people still did not believe that I could compete at the major Division I level. My goals were never for them, and I didn't care what they thought or believed.

That year was a defining moment not only in my sports career but in my life. It was a culmination of what I had already been taught to be true and what I believed, as I truly realized that when other people had low expectations of me, their opinions were irrelevant. All that really mattered was what I thought was possible, what I was willing to work for, and what I believed I was capable of doing. I drew so many experiences later in life from the feelings and the thoughts of those early mornings; on many of those mornings I would literally be attempting to beat the alarm clock in getting up. As I think back about how my mind worked during my junior year, all I can think about is how much of an obsession becoming the best possible player that I could was to me. I remember thinking how I may not have been waking up early enough because someone in another time zone was waking up before me, and thinking that there was no way that person wanted that spot on a major Division I team more than I did.

I remember going to sleep relatively early for a high school junior, at 9:00 p.m. or 9:30 p.m. When I would talk to my classmates about what time I went to sleep, they'd laugh at me and make fun of me for turning in so early. The high school basketball season lasted from late September through February, so most of the time it was relatively cold outside, even in Baton Rouge, Louisiana. When the alarm would sound in the morning, especially early on during this process, I can remember thinking, "Man, these covers are nice and warm. It would really be nice to stay in bed this morning. No one will really know the difference." Those were the times when I started molding myself into the type of person who not only was willing, but looked forward to doing the things that most other people wouldn't do. I truly took pride in the fact that I was outworking everybody I knew, and that it wasn't even a close call. That year I also stopped running cross-country. I had been running for five years at that point, since I was in the fifth grade, and my cross-country experience had also added to my mentally tough mind-set. What cross-country did for me was give me the physical stamina to keep going. I remember thinking that there was no way that anyone who was on the court with me was in as good of shape as I was and that I could run all day. There was absolutely no way that they could keep up with me for the entire game, in my mind. They may very well have been faster, quicker, and stronger, but they didn't have the stamina and mental fortitude. The mental side of what cross-country gave me may have been even more important. These were the thoughts that said, "Keep going! Keep going! Pick up the pace to that tree. Catch that guy in front of you and separate from him. Don't let him know you're tired. Modify your breathing as you run by him so he doesn't even hear you." These were the types of thoughts that would be going through my mind as I ran, and I carried them over to the basketball court. I would never put my hands on my knees during a game. My way of thinking was that if I don't stop, eventually you will, and that's when I'll beat you. I saw myself as the Energizer bunny.

My junior year, we actually got a new coach, John Freeman, who was new to the area. He wasn't aware of the mentality of many of those in southern Louisiana and thought that as long as he played the best players and won, everything would be okay. With the bulk of the starters playing football, we got off to a slow start, but as our team rounded out in the early part of the season before we started district play, things started to come together, and I knew we would have a great season. We had a very talented team, filled with veteran guys, my junior year. Troy Williams, Kyle Pourciau, Jeff Nelson, Michael Selders, myself, and my younger brother Elliott made up the starting five and the sixth man that year. We had a great group of guys, a great chemistry, an understanding of everyone's roles, and a coach who genuinely wanted to see his team do well, not only for himself, but also for his players. I remember that year as an extremely fun time where we won a lot and had a great team, but didn't achieve quite what we should have with the talent we had. Looking back on it, I realize that a lack of structure played somewhat of a role in that. We had a lot of fun, and Coach Freeman gave us a lot of freedom. He didn't yell and scream, but the level of accountability was probably not where it could have been to help us grow as players. The reality in my mind was that I needed that year with John Freeman, though. Despite the fact that as a team we didn't perform quite to our level of capable play, Coach Freeman believed in my ability so much that I gained the in-game confidence that got me recognized even more and gave me the belief that I was one of best players in the state. We should have won the state championship my junior year, but we lost in the third round to the eventual champions. My emergence as an elite player in the state started that year.

That summer was a continuation of the work that I had done through-out my junior year. After losing in the playoffs to Springfield during junior year, I took no days off. I went right back to work without flinching or saying I was worn out, tired, or any other excuse. It had become a way of life. The only downtime I can remember during that summer was when my father took my brothers and me to Egypt for ten days. It was a life-changing trip that I will never forget, but I remember being ready to get home to see all the letters from schools that had piled up and to get back to work. I had five on-campus school visits that I had the option to take. During our high school summer league that year, LSU's new coach, John Brady, and his assistant and head recruiter, Butch Pierre, would drop in to see me play periodically. There were many other coaches whom I was talking to and thinking about. Perry Clark at Tulane, Tic Price at Memphis, and Seth Greenberg at South Florida were the top three choices, among others. Outside of LSU, Arkansas and Nolan Richardson were the only other SEC schools that showed a great deal of interest and that I remotely considered. The real reason that I ever considered any school other than LSU was due to the way the staff of the Fighting Tigers were pursuing me—or the lack of pursuit, in my mind. I felt that I wasn't being given enough attention by the school in my backyard. Looking back on it now, I think of something I heard Art Williams, the billionaire and founder of A. L. Williams, the precursor for Primerica, say: "Everybody has a flashing sign on their chest that says, 'Make me feel special, make me feel good, say something good to me, I want to be somebody!'" That's EXACTLY how I felt, and those other schools I mentioned earlier were wooing me more than LSU seemed to be. I didn't want the LSU guys to offer me a scholarship solely based on my father's association with the school, but rather because of what they truly believed I could do on and off the court to add value to their team and the overall well-being of the program. Looking back, I may have had a slightly inflated view of myself, but I truly saw myself as a guy whom a program could be built around, based on a few things. I was what coaches call a "character guy," someone who had a strong moral compass and was focused on doing the right things on and off the court. Also, I could play and had a tremendous upside.

I worked hard that summer, spent a lot of time in the weight room, and even grew more. By the start of my senior season, I was a legitimate six foot four and was stronger than I had ever been. I was quicker, faster, and jumping higher than I ever had. And thanks to my parents' decision to hold me back in kindergarten, even though I started my senior season at seventeen years old, I was eighteen for most of the year, which made all the difference in the world for me physically. All high school basketball players being recruited by Division I schools are offered the opportunity to take five "official visits." I never took my official visits. My mind-set was that if the school I truly wanted to attend offered me a full ride, I didn't want to drag that school along, nor did I want to placate the other schools that were offering me scholarships and take advantage of visits they could use for others who were seriously considering signing with them. Deep in my heart, if not my mind, I wanted to play for LSU, and once LSU extended me a letter of intent during the early signing period of my senior year, prior to the season, I took advantage of it. Prior to my senior season, in a small ceremony in U-High's library, I accomplished what had been a dream of mine for eleven years, since I was six years old, of following in my father's footsteps and signing a letter of intent to play basketball on a full scholarship for the Fighting Tigers of Louisiana State University. It was the culmination of a lot of hard work, dedication, coachability, and focus. I remember that even after signing with LSU—or maybe it was because I had signed with LSU—I played with an expectation and swagger that bordered on being cocky my senior year; I wanted to prove to everyone that LSU hadn't made a mistake.

We switched head coaches again my senior year, taking the number of different head coaches during my four-year high school career to three. Ari Fisher became our head coach during my last year. He was a guy who had played at U-High himself; he was "different," but he was a passionate student of the game. He was someone who respected the hard work and dedication that were my trademark. Ari was only twenty-seven when he got the head coach job at U-High. He was a relatively young first-time head coach who came into the job with his own ideas, like most coaches do, I would assume. The year prior, he had been an assistant with Dale Brown at LSU briefly for one year prior to Coach Brown's retirement, and he was anxious to take his alma mater back to the championship glory it had seen during the 1980s. U-High had won the state championship in 1983 and 1984 and had been the runner-up in 1985 and 1986 under the great coach Gerald Furr. Because of my size by my senior year and my ability to play all five positions very well during high school, Ari wanted to use me all over the floor and get more people involved in the offense, which in theory was a great idea. The only problem with that idea was that even though I was by far the best scorer on our team, I also was the best facilitator and passer, and the offense flowed best when it ran through me and when I was able to create more opportunities for my teammates. We had a good team my senior year—we weren't as talented top to bottom as we were my junior year, but we were still good enough to contend for the state title. I look back on those junior and senior seasons, and see that I learned the difference between running a program and coaching for a season. This also played a role in my success after I left U-High. I remember the first team meeting we had, where Ari gave us our team motto, "areté," which means "excellence" in Greek. The fact that we had a defined team motto that encompassed how Ari expected us to compete and perform was different than anything I had dealt with. He had specific practice plans for every practice that were typed out with the specific amount of time for each; he had everything set up in a very uniform way. Despite the fact that I didn't agree with all of his ideas as to how we could maximize the talent on our team, I totally respected what he wanted to do as the head coach, as well as the time, effort, and energy that he put into being and becoming a great coach for himself, for our team, and for his program in general. I related to Ari because we were both basketball junkies and gym rats—guys who loved everything about the game, from the history to the nuances of different offenses.

My senior campaign ended up being a successful one from a numbers perspective. I had career high averages across the board: twenty-seven points, 9.5 rebounds, and eight assists a game, as well as shooting 54 percent from the field, which was great for a volume shooter who wasn't a center or power forward. I also shot well from behind the three-point line and free-throw line. I stepped my game up even more in district play when it mattered most, as I took my scoring average up to slightly over thirty per game. I hated that I hadn't been able to bring the title back to University High that had been gone for fourteen years, but I was happy about my last two years of basketball. I led the city in scoring average my senior year and garnered a host of other awards, including district MVP, all-district first team, all-metro, all-state first team, and an honorable mention as a McDonald's All-American. I was excited about entering the next chapter of my life and secure in my ability to determine my destiny based on persistence and hard work. Having accomplished my goals all along the way, I was extremely confident that I could truly do whatever I wanted and make an immediate impact as a freshman in the SEC on LSU's team that next year. I could not have imagined what the next five years would mean to me: the challenges, the triumphs, the growth opportunities, and how they would impact and make a difference in my life.

WSTM LESSONS LEARNED

1. Ask yourself the question, "Have I done the necessary work to truly EXPECT success? Do I really deserve to win? Am I operating like a THIEF (expecting something for nothing), a GAMBLER (hoping to win the jackpot without putting much effort forward), or a CHAMPION (doing whatever it takes to succeed)?" Answer the question as objectively and honestly as you can. Remember, if you can't be objectively honest with yourself, you'll have a very tough time becoming successful.

2. Remember that everyone wants to be made to feel special. Always keep that in mind and go out of your way to practice that amazing skill! That's what true CHARISMA is.

3. There's a difference between doing what's necessary to build a program and being successful for a single season. Decide where you want to be in terms of building a winning program as it relates to your life, determine the price, and go to work.

Chapter 9

❖

THE THREE COMMON DENOMINATORS OF SUCCESS: COACHABILITY, FOCUS, AND WORK ETHIC

It's the things you do when you don't have to that will always determine when it's too late to do anything about it. —Anonymous

F-O-C-U-S: Follow One Course Until Successful. —Anonymous

You can't get ahead, stayin' in bed! —Collis Temple Sr.

After becoming a relatively successful businessman and receiving opportunities to speak all over North America, I've often been asked by people to articulate why I've been able to experience whatever success that I have in my life thus far. This question has put me in a position where I've learned to condense it down to a few simple points. At the end of the day, anyone who has succeeded in anything at a remotely high level would probably admit that it was relatively SIMPLE. I would agree. That being said, I wouldn't underestimate the statement of "it was SIMPLE." I've definitely learned that *simple* and *easy* are two totally different things. The reason that I chose to put this chapter at this point in the book is because it was during this first part of my life that these concepts and this mentality were built in my mind. It was during this time in my life when I realized, "Winning is not hard—losing is just very easy!"

I've broken down my explanation for success into what I call the three common denominators. Dictionary.com's definition of *denominator* is "something shared, or held in common; standard." This is exactly how I use the term because everyone who's had success in anything has in some shape or form practiced these ideas personally. You've probably heard the saying "success leaves clues" and that "there are common threads of success woven into successful people." I totally and 100 percent believe both of those statements, and that's why I think the common denominators of success are a very simple methodology that, for me at least, have clearly defined MY success and could help anyone willing to apply them to become more successful as well.

THE THREE COMMON DENOMINATORS OF SUCCESS:

1. COACHABILITY
2. FOCUS
3. WORK ETHIC

COACHABILITY

The first of the common denominators is COACHABILITY, which I would define as the ability to seek out, accept, internalize, and apply information that is given by someone who may be a mentor or expert in the area you're looking to excel in. People who are coachable can easily be discovered because they operate with a certain mentality. Those who are coachable never think they know everything; their mentality is NOT "I already know" but rather "I NEED TO GROW." There are several parts of true coachability. The first step to total coachability is SEEKING IT OUT. You should SEEK OUT whatever it is that will help you in becoming more successful in the desired area that you're striving to excel in. The best place to start seeking is with MENTORS who have accomplished what you want to accomplish. Those who have been successful before us want to ADMIRE someone and INSPIRE others. The best feel almost an obligation to teach and give their knowledge to those who want to achieve higher levels of greatness in particular fields. That being said, successful people didn't become the best by being idle, so these people are also usually extremely busy, and although they don't mind giving advice, they usually have to be sought out. The high achievers usually won't voluntarily drop nuggets in your lap while you sit and wait. Far too often, I've experienced scenarios where people have believed that they were coachable, yet they wait to be coached versus seeking that coaching out. Most people need to be more assertive when it comes to being coached and wanting to grow and get better.

When it comes to the second part of coachability, ACCEPTING the advice given, it's important that a person doesn't have thin skin and can acknowledge the mentor's advice for what it is—a clear and honest assessment of what should be done to achieve greater success. I learned this from a mentor: "WEAK people NEED to be told what to do, and STRONG people WANT to be told what to do." The bottom line is, those who have been entrusted with working with, teaching, training, and developing others need to explain to those individuals what's next on their success journey. People who don't accept coaching are usually those who don't keep mentors for long. If they've chosen quality mentors and don't accept coaching, they usually don't achieve much success either. A great mentor understands that it's not about simply barking directions, but really explaining the "whys" behind these directives to help their mentees understand how to duplicate the process once they are charged with doing it without the mentor around. Many times, part of accepting the advice is gaining an understanding of why that may be the case. I didn't say total agreement on why, just understanding from the mentor's point of view. If agreement may not be met early on during the process, it's often the case that it occurs later on, after the mentee has experienced the full process. Remember, the mentee is the one who asked for the help and hopefully sought it out. If the mentee was fully aware and understood what the mentor was attempting to teach him or her prior to being taught, the question would be, "Why would the mentor be necessary in the first place?" Paraphrasing an Albert Einstein quote, "We cannot reach a higher level of understanding with our current mind-set. Our current mind-set has gotten us where we currently are." As I learned from one of my major mentors, Bill Whittle, "if you thought like I thought, you'd have what I have." That being said, you may not totally agree with all the things your mentor coaches you to do. Once the mentees have reached the point of understanding the "why" and accepting it, they have reached the INTERNALIZING phase of coachability, which is taking the advice as their own mentality and mind-set.

The last and most important phase in the process of true coachability is APPLICATION. Great mentors don't have a lot of time to waste, and when they mentor someone, unapplied information that leads to nowhere for the mentee constitutes wasted time on the mentor's part. What's the point of asking for the advice of someone who's experienced great success if you don't plan on applying the information that the person's giving? The most successful mentees apply the idea of doing "that, and then some" when it comes to applying the advice given by their mentors. Whatever they're coached to do, not only do they strive to accomplish what the mentor has advised, but they strive for even greater levels by putting out the extra effort and energy, doing a little bit more, and spending a little bit more time. The idea of application at a greater level is one that isn't new or foreign to the greatest performers. It's how they become great. The mentees who want to outperform and maximize their potential must begin to make a habit of going the extra mile. "How you do anything is how you do everything." Because that is definitely the case, why not start the habit of going that extra mile in the process of being mentored and applying the information you have been given? If you've ever heard the age-old saying "KNOWLEDGE IS POWER," you've both heard correctly and been taught incorrectly. I say that because KNOWLEDGE without APPLICATION is truly STUPIDITY! If a person KNOWS better and does not take the necessary action to DO BETTER, what would we call that person? (You said it—I didn't.) I've adopted the ideal that APPLIED KNOWLEDGE IS POWER! It makes ALL the difference in the world!

Once a person has begun experiencing success, it's also key to have the WISDOM to stay HUMBLE and continue to LISTEN and GROW. This is usually harder for those who start to have success than those who don't, so be aware of that, and don't fall into the trap that success sometimes sets for people who haven't experienced it often or who may not be ready to accept the responsibility that comes with success.

From a practical perspective, I have had several opportunities to sharpen and refine my ability to be coached. My involvement in athletics obviously played a great role in getting me ready for success as a result of accepting and yielding to great coaching, but also growing up with parents like I had who coached every day in life situations prepared me. I first gained a personal understanding of coachability through my participation in athletics and playing basketball for my father in elementary school. I also gained a lot of appreciation for the idea of being coachable from the many instances of working with my younger brother, Elliott, for my dad's construction and demolition company, CT and Sons Construction, during the sweltering summers in southern Louisiana. At CT and Sons, I worked in many different capacities, from helping with all the things necessary when moving houses, to mixing paint and painting rental houses, to taking nails out of cypress wood to be reused, to stacking pallets of bricks, and more. Looking at me now, you would probably not ascertain that I would know a lot about these types of things, but I've done it all. I can remember an instance during one of the many renovations to the house that we grew up in when my father told Elliott and me to move a pallet of bricks from where they were to another location that was only about twenty feet away. I was about eleven, and Elliott was nine. At the time he asked us, we weren't doing anything in particular, and that was the problem. He never wanted us to be idle, and I could remember not knowing why he wanted us to move the bricks, but knowing that the fact that I didn't know at that time was in no shape or form justification for not quickly taking the action and starting to do the work with a smile and in an enthusiastic manner. My parents would take the time to explain why it was necessary to do the things that they were "strongly suggesting." Of course there were instances where they didn't explain everything at the specific moment when they told me to do it, but if I ever asked why it was necessary, it was clearly explained in a way that I could process it, accept it, and make it part of how I lived my life. I truly internalized the lessons my parents imparted because they didn't just TELL me; they TRAINED and EDUCATED me as to why I needed to do things in a certain manner. With my dad, everything was a quiz, and he had us in constant learning mode while he was always in teaching mode. I was extremely fortunate to not have parents of the "do it because I said so" type, but parents who would take the time to explain to us the reasoning for the suggestions that they were making.

It's my belief that part of why some teenagers rebel or act out once they leave their parents' home and go in an opposite direction from what they have been told to do is because they haven't been truly made aware of the "whys" and the reasoning for taking certain actions. I haven't had the privilege of parenting a teenager yet, but I'm looking forward to what I've been told is an interesting experience in patience. Coachability is obviously key in athletics and also in business success, but the place that I've experienced the greatest learning is from being parented. As excited as I am about my businesses, the coaching opportunities that I'm the most excited about come in the form of my family and helping my children navigate their lives' journeys and achieve the goals they set for themselves.

FOCUS

The next denominator for success is a person's ability to focus. Focus is defined by Dictionary.com as "a central point, as of attraction, attention, or activity." I define focus as the ability to stay locked in on a goal or dream, regardless of LIFE happening around you. It's a definite fact that LIFE will occur as you pursue your goals and the things that you want to accomplish. It also is a fact that those who figure out how to navigate those distractions and achieve success anyway are the ones who will experience everything that goal accomplishment has to offer, which is A LOT! In a world where it is so easy to be distracted, the ability to stay locked in and focused has become more and more important. I remember early on in my life when I'd get involved with a project or get an idea to do something in my mind. My mom would describe me as having "tunnel vision." In most cases she was saying that somewhat as a negative, because during my ninth- and tenth-grade years, she thought I should have a had a more well-rounded high school existence outside of school and sports, even though she realized how serious I was about accomplishing my goals. Once I got into the business world, I learned a quote from Art Williams, the multibillionaire, who—in addition to changing the lives of millions upon millions of people—has become a personal acquaintance. Art said, "The losers in life think that the winners don't deal with the same challenges that they deal with."

Whether you consider yourself a religious or spiritual person or not, you have probably heard of the concept of "praying without ceasing." The Bible talks about "praying without ceasing," but if we were to translate that literally, anyone who did it would not live very long, because to do anything without ceasing requires that you do NOTHING else, including eating, sleeping, and the like. In my mind, it's obvious that this means to FOCUS on something with intensity. There are always those who interpret the Bible literally, but think about it—if a person truly prayed without ceasing, he or she would not be able to eat, sleep, or do almost anything else. It is my EXTREMELY NOVICE opinion, in relation to the Bible, that it just means to stay focused and think about the thing that you want to come to fruition. Prayer is DEFINITELY a form of focus, and, unfortunately, so is worrying. Fortunately for me, there aren't many things that cause me to worry, but many people aren't like that. In my estimation, I know that there are certain things that I can control, and I focus on doing what I need to do to control those things. For me, God's in control of the rest, which means, why should I worry about it?

Success in ANYTHING is all about PROGRAMMING ourselves, and for many of us, REPROGRAMMING is necessary to succeed. I was raised setting goals and, without realizing it, saying affirmations to myself. My dad taught me how to set my goals and then suggested that I write them down on paper and put them up somewhere in my room where I would see them and be reminded of them every day. That became something that I did with regularity starting in the sixth grade. This was definitely something that helped me improve my ability to focus because it was in front of me every day. Once again, going back to coaching, he helped goal setting make sense to me by explaining with an analogy. I had just started running cross-country, and his example was that it would be tough to win a race if I had no clue where the finish line was, especially if I planned on running out front and leading the pack. Just as when leading the pack in a race with an unknown finish line, it's extremely tough to accomplish a goal you haven't set yet.

Goal setting is of PARAMOUNT importance when it comes to a person's ability to focus. Without SHORT- and LONG-TERM goals that are both time sensitive and measurable, you don't have a track to run on when it comes to goal accomplishment.

Another point that must be duly noted regarding FOCUSING is that when it comes to blocking out distractions and staying zeroed in on a goal, the distractions can be GOOD or BAD. Getting married, the birth of a child, having experienced great success, or perhaps accomplishing the last major goal you set—ALL of these are great examples of things that may very well serve as POSITIVE DISTRACTIONS on the way to the accomplishment of a higher goal. If you haven't reached what your ultimate goal was to begin with, anything that may take your focus away from putting forth the effort to accomplish that goal could be considered a DISTRACTION.

Early on in my life, I learned about the concept of FOCUS from gaining knowledge in relation to the power of goal setting. Thanks to my parents' instruction, goal setting became an extremely important part of my life. I really started zeroing in on the authority over accomplishments that setting goals gave me in the fifth grade, when I would set goals and actually start hitting them. At first I started setting goals in sports, but I quickly realized that the concept applied to my academic career as well, along with everything else in my life. Imagine the mental strength and confidence associated with being only eleven and having the knowledge that I could truly do whatever I wanted to if I could write it on paper and be willing to work toward accomplishing it. My belief became that "it's hard to hit a goal I have not set," so why not set it and shoot for it?

I remember being a five-foot-seven, 125-pound, very nonathletic, puny, but abnormally driven and mentally tough freshman who wanted to earn a college scholarship to play basketball at a major Division I university, specifically LSU. I set a long-term goal to earn a college basketball scholarship four years from then. My short-term goal was to earn a spot on the varsity basketball team, which, at University High, was not normal at the time. I followed through on the goal-setting formula I had been coached to follow by my mom and dad: I wrote those goals down and then posted them on the mirror in my room, where I'd see them every morning. Three and a half years later, I was sitting in U-High's library signing a letter of intent to play basketball and attend Louisiana State University. It was funny to hear my mom tell me that I was too "tunnel visioned." She wasn't like many moms probably are, saying I didn't need to get my hopes up or that I couldn't accomplish the things that I was setting out to do, but she did think I was too young to be so serious and so focused on the accomplishment of one thing. As supportive as she was in EVERY way when it came to me pursuing my goals, her mind-set was that I shouldn't limit myself that early in my life to the achievement of only one central goal. She believed that I was capable of excelling in several areas outside of just sports. Looking back, I smile when I think about two things:

1. Having the ability to be "tunnel visioned" when it came to accomplishing my goals has helped me so much that it's amazing.
2. She was probably right about me limiting myself at the time, but the accomplishment of that definite major goal gave me the confidence to attempt and do other things with a high amount of assurance in my ability to achieve whatever I set my mind to.

When it comes to staying locked in and FOCUSED, the partner of goal setting is AFFIRMATIONS. The definition, according to Dictionary. com, of affirmations that I like best is "the assertion that something exists or is true." Goals help chart the course, and AFFIRMATIONS continually breathe the life of belief into your mind that the goals you've set can, will, and actually have ALREADY happened and that you just need to bring them into their natural form and existence. This was an extremely EXCITING revelation for me when I truly realized the power of affirmations in helping me to remain focused. AFFIRMATIONS help keep you locked in on your goals and the things you're striving to accomplish.

The first form of affirmations that I remember saying to myself were done unconsciously while I was in the driveway shooting basketball. I would play an entire game, commentating the entire thing from start to finish, and it'd usually end up with me either hitting a game-winning shot at the buzzer or having been fouled at the free-throw line, down one with two free throws and no time left on the clock. Oddly enough, I experienced these same scenarios several times in my basketball career in high school and college during game situations, where I hit big shots at clutch moments in the game to win the game for our team. There is ZERO doubt in my mind that the mental preparation that took place at an early age prepared me to succeed under pressure the way that I would later in my life as those situations presented themselves.

Today, in business, my affirmations are specific, on purpose, and always written down! Discipline plays an obvious role in anyone's success if that person is succeeding at a high level, but as one of my mentors, Bill Whittle, says, "When you've got someone or something that's important enough to you, you'll find the discipline to do what's necessary to achieve your goal." My favorite quote about discipline actually plays down the importance of discipline, interestingly enough: "You don't have a discipline problem; you've got a desire problem. If you wanted something bad enough, you'd get the discipline necessary to accomplish it." That's another gem from Bill Whittle. People won't be able to focus or maintain the necessary discipline if they aren't affirming and believing that they can truly achieve the things they've set out to do and accomplish.

WORK ETHIC

The third and arguably the most important of the three common denominators of success is WORK ETHIC. The definition of *work ethic* is "a belief in the moral benefit and importance of work and its inherent ability to strengthen character." I LOVE this definition, and it's dead-on for me. In addition, 2 Thessalonians 3:10 says, "The one who is unwilling to work shall not eat." In my mind, it cannot be made much more simple and plain than that.

I was extremely fortunate to have two phenomenal examples in my parents, whom I grew up watching and who worked very hard. In my mind, it's just as important to note that as I watched my parents work hard, I also watched them enjoy life and have control over their lives. The conversation about them being successful entrepreneurs and business owners is for another time, but I truly believe that the reason hard work gets a bad rap under certain circumstances is because young adults who've watched their parents work hard and still not have anything or still not live the "American dream" decide they won't buy into a lie. I learned that as long as you're in the right vehicle, hard work pays off EVERY TIME! That was a strong belief that was burned into my brain by my parents, especially my dad.

My mom's work ethic came from her watching her parents hustle every day and have a great deal of respect in the community. Her belief in a strong work ethic, coupled with her intense desire to be somebody and want something more, propelled her to success.

My dad was TRAINED from an early age to understand the moral benefit and importance of work and its inherent ability to strengthen character. It was seared into his brain by my grandfather, Collis Sr., that you "can't get ahead staying in bed!" and that the only way to succeed at a high level was to "work like a slave, and think like a master" —thus the name of this book.

The belief that I couldn't and wouldn't truly win without hard work was burned into my subconscious mind so deeply that it is as much a part of me as my physical limbs. I remember hearing my dad say, "Wake up, Collis! Remember, you can't get ahead staying in bed!" I would jump up and get moving because I was always taught that I needed to be and wanted to be AHEAD, out front, leading, winning. It's amazing how that positive brainwashing has had such a profound impact on my life, but thinking about it, it really shouldn't be that much of a surprise. The reason I say it shouldn't be that much of a surprise is because the opposite brainwashing yields similar results in the opposite direction, and unfortunately there are many more examples of those detrimental results.

My experiences in athletics were a strong PROVER of my dad's motto that you "can't get ahead stay' in bed." I started out waking up early in the morning with him to go run around the lakes near our home, and it would still be dark outside. Then it got to the point, while I was still in elementary school, where I'd be running around the lakes on my own without him. Early on, I remember the thoughts that would go through my mind in relation to me waking up early and running, working on my shooting in the driveway, or whatever I was focusing on doing. I would get to school, and when we were about to play basketball at recess, I would truly think, "I've been practicing; there's no way that these guys can play with me. I'm way better than all of them. They haven't worked as hard at this as I have." I know that sounds weird—it sounds weird to me as I say it some twenty-five years later—but I remember thinking like that. When it came to cross-country, I remember thinking the same things, and when I was in the seventh grade competing with—and, in most cases, beating—the guys on the varsity team, I would just be thinking that they couldn't compete with me, and it didn't even matter that they were older and stronger. I developed a belief that HARD WORK was a GREAT EQUALIZER and, in many cases, the GREAT SEPARATOR! Even today, I cannot stay in bed past a certain time as a residual effect of my programming. They don't come very often at all, but I may have a day, such as a holiday, when there's not anything in particular on my schedule, but I still don't feel comfortable sleeping past a certain time of day. I have the mind-set that I'm missing something, or that someone else is working while I'm sleeping. I can't stand either of those thoughts; they make my skin crawl, and as a result I can't stay asleep.

C. B. Temple was also the architect of the idea that you'd better "work like a slave, and think like a master." This painted such a powerful picture in my mind early on. It was a saying that my dad introduced me after the saying that you "can't get ahead staying in bed." I can only speculate that it was because of the seriousness of the statements. Most slaves, of course, would be required to work from before it was light outside in the morning until past sundown in the evening, and that's how I was trained to believe. The other side of the saying, "think like a master," referred to the future planning and the idea of thinking ahead and laying out a course to achieve success. I remember not liking the statement at first when I thought about it literally, but once I grasped the essence of the statement on a deeper level, it became the adage that I would live by.

By the time I got into business, I had realized that these common denominators applied across the board and that they weren't only applicable in the world of academics and athletics. Just as in anything else, I realized that the most successful people would find a WAY, whereas the unsuccessful people were far too often finding an EXCUSE. Everyone deals with different external circumstances that they can very easily allow to cause their defeat, but the biggest obstacles to most people's success are their internal hang-ups and hindrances.

Early in life I was programmed to believe in these three common denominators. I was taught that these three things, along with my belief in God, could yield me all the positive results that I wanted. Once I got out of school, was done playing ball, and was moving into the world of real life and business, I was told by Bill Whittle that "God puts the grapes in our reach and not in our hand." I believe that statement totally sums up the concept of the three common denominators of success. We have to remain coachable to DIRECTIVES (the Bible) we've been given in order to live the type of life we want and to the mind's VOICE (God) that nudges us to be better and do more. We must remain FOCUSED on the goals and dreams (grapes) we have in spite of the distractions and preoccupations that may come up, pulling our attention away from the things at hand. Last, we must do the HARD WORK (reach) necessary to earn success. The things we want are there, but God blesses our efforts. Do you DESERVE to experience SUCCESS?

WSTM LESSONS LEARNED

1. Once you've established a desire to accomplish something in a specific area, ask yourself these important questions:

   a. "Do I have a mentor in this area of my life who has done, or is doing, what I want to accomplish?"

   b. "Am I being 100 percent coachable, or am I being selectively coachable?"

2. Do you have knowledge that you are not properly applying to get the results that you desire? If so, move forward with the right mind-set and start applying that information.

3. Take the time to explain the "whys" to your children. It makes all the difference in the world.

4. Reassess your connection between work ethic and success. If there are some mental shifts and adjustments that need to be made, take care of making those necessary changes so they don't serve as roadblocks toward accomplishment of your goals.

Part II

MY COLLEGE EXPERIENCE

Chapter 10

"USE THE HATERS AS MOTIVATORS"

*Life is too short to hang around cynical
people. Find people who will believe in
your dreams and celebrate your victories. —Joel Osteen*

*They didn't call me, they didn't equip me, and
they definitely can't stop me! —Anonymous*

*If you don't have another hater by the end of the
day, you aren't doing enough! —Katt Williams*

I'm a total believer in the power of positive energy being a greater force than negative energy in EVERY INSTANCE; that being said, I must admit that one of the several motivating factors for me as I strived to accomplish many of my goals and achieve higher levels of success was proving wrong those who had doubted me. While I was growing up, during middle school and at the beginning of my high school career, I was not always the odds-on favorite to succeed at a very high level in the athletic realm. My greatest strength, especially early on, was my work ethic. Even once I finally started growing—and despite the numbers I was putting up my junior and senior seasons in high school at University High—for some reason, there were still those who doubted my ability to truly compete in the environment of major college basketball. I say "for some reason" fully understanding that there will always be doubters, negative people, and naysayers. It's just unfortunate that everyone won't be happy for you, but I learned early on to USE IT to my advantage versus allowing it to cloud the clear vision I had for achieving success at a higher level.

My mentality about "using the haters as motivators" started early on in my life. I remember overhearing conversations that my dad would have with older men while I was a clumsy but determined ten-, eleven-, and twelve-year-old about how he figured that I would grow into my body and play major college basketball and probably end up being a professional. The other men would laugh at my dad's over-assertions of his son's extremely limited ability. I remember men who I thought believed in me and had my best interest at heart laughing out loud at the idea that I could excel at a high level as an athlete. I can vividly recall thinking, "I'll prove them all WRONG!" I must admit, though, as focused as I was on proving them wrong, I was more focused on proving my dad right! That goes back to my focus on positive energy over negative energy.

Looking back and thinking about it, and knowing my dad, that very well may have been a part of his plan as well. Who knows? He was always helping me find motivation in so many different types of ways. Letting me overhear conversations about people doubting my ability may have been part of a master plan that he had. He knew that he and my mother gave me so much positive affirmation and legitimate praise that he had constructed my mind to not only handle the negative things that people would say, but to use them as fuel and motivation.

In terms of success, I learned at an early age that all I needed was one person in my corner who believed in me. That's probably why I have been able to achieve at such a high level, because I've always had two people—both of my parents—and once I got a taste of success, I really didn't need anyone else to show me because I had built such a strong belief in myself and my own ability that I felt unstoppable.

When I was in junior high, Mark Young was a local Baton Rouge high school basketball standout from the legendary McKinley High School. He later had a nice college career at Kansas State and was an NBA journeyman for a couple of years. Mark was in high school and was volunteering as a coach during the Sports Academy House League. The way the House League worked was that after two Saturdays of the coaches at all the different levels evaluating the talent pool based on drill work and pick-up games in a controlled environment, they would pick teams to play games on Saturdays for the next two months. I was about twelve years old and was a pretty good player, despite not being the strongest or most athletic, and when it came time for the draft, Mark drafted a young lady named Jessica Shanklin ahead of me. Now, I must admit that Jessica was easily one of the best players in the House League—she was the Seimone Augustus of Baton Rouge before Seimone came of age a few years later—but in my mind she wasn't where I was as a player. Still today, when I bring it up, Mark holds on to the claim that he needed a true point guard, and I was more of a score-first point guard. I think he says that now to save face with me about the fact that he really just thought she was a better overall player than I was back then. I don't think I will ever forget Mark doing that, and even though he and I laugh about it now and are friends today, the first thing I still think about when I see him or talk to him is, "He actually picked Jessica Shanklin over me in the House League draft." I know it's weird, but that's just how my mind works, and Mark's someone I consider a friend!

We all know of or have personally experienced instances where kids, being kids, have been harsh or made jokes. Many of those instances for me revolved around me playing ball in middle school basketball games when the opposing fans (many of whom were older than middle school) would be taunting me with "URKEL, URKEL," calling me the name of the popular 1990s nerd on the hit sitcom *Family Matters*. This was because I would actually wear my pants on my waist with my shirt tucked in, and many times, my shorts were barely at my knees. I also wore goggles when I played because I wore glasses, and this was before I got contacts. I remember not caring how I looked but being totally focused on how I played, how hard I worked, and outplaying everyone else on the floor. I was driven by a strong desire to be the best and compete at the highest level that I could; anyone who voiced an opinion that wasn't in alignment with my thoughts was, in my mind, a motivator for greater success.

Once I got to high school and was still not the most imposing physical specimen but had developed into a really good player, several upperclassman, some on the team and others who weren't, would call me selfish or say that I wasn't as good as I thought I was. I never believed them or gave credence to the things they were saying. I truly understood that they realized they couldn't compete in any way other than by trying to get in my head and that it was only a matter of time before they'd come over to my side, and even if they never did, it was perfectly okay.

I remember loving to watch videos about Michael Jordan: *Come Fly with Me*, *Michael Jordan: Airtime*, and *Above and Beyond*. I would listen to him talk about people not thinking that he'd be good enough to compete, and I would draw parallels between his career and the things I was dealing with. Still to this day, my favorite series of movies are the Rocky movies. I'm just a huge fan of the underdog concept and the idea of overcoming odds to become something great, something inspiring, something unbelievable. Watching these Jordan highlight videos and movies like Rocky gave me the belief that I could truly use the negative things that people said as fuel to become better. I knew that as long as I believed I could accomplish the things I was setting out to do and there was one person who believed in my ability, I could accomplish whatever I wanted to. I was extremely fortunate that I had plenty of positive reinforcement from my family, which was more than enough, but I must admit that I've always had a somewhat sick desire to want to prove wrong those who doubt me. It's important to note that I don't allow my desire to "use the haters as motivators" consume me or take up very much of my thought process, but if there's an option between using it as a driving force and allowing it to slow my progress, it definitely is a motivating factor.

THE SUMMER BEFORE MY COLLEGE CAREER

Going into my freshman year at LSU, I was extremely excited and anxious! Coming off of a solid senior year, I was going into the Louisiana high school all-star game during the summer of 1998 with all the best players from the state, with high expectations. That year there was an abundance of talent in the state from my class of graduates. Almost everyone in that game had signed Division I scholarships. There were three guys on the East team with me who had signed with LSU: Brad Bridgewater of Pointe Coupee Central, who was a raw but ultra-athletic six-foot-eight power forward; Marqus LeDoux of Parkview Baptist High School, who had played with my dad's AAU team early during my AAU career and who was a smooth, unassuming six-foot-eight power forward; and Jermaine Williams, whom I had known since I was six years old, was a good friend, and who had also helped build the Parkview Baptist High School bas-ketball dynasty. Jermaine was a six-foot-six, defensive-minded, and ex-tremely unselfish shooting guard/small forward. Marqus and Jermaine were both more highly recruited than I was.

On the West team was Nick Sinville, the six-foot-eight power forward who had beat me out for Class 2A player-of-the-year honors the previous year and had signed to play with Tulane in New Orleans. Also featured on the West squad were Brandon Dean, the ridiculously explosive, high-scoring, six-foot point guard who had signed with Arkansas, and Teddy Gipson, the six-foot-three, quick and silky smooth-shooting guard who had also signed with Arkansas. The prize recruit of Louisiana was also featured on the West team. Stromile Swift had attended Fair Park High School in Shreveport, Louisiana, and was one of the top-five players in the country, having been named 1998 Louisiana Player of the Year and First Team McDonald's All-American. LSU had landed this highly rated prospect, and he was raising the level of excitement surrounding LSU basketball again. He was a six-foot-nine, ultra-athletic power forward who was the main reason that the 1998 game was such a highly attended all-star game. To top things off, the game was to be played on LSU's campus in the PMAC (Pete Maravich Assembly Center), where five of us from that game would be playing the following year. John Brady, LSU's head coach, was at the game as well. Brady was going into his second year and the first where he had been able to recruit for an entire recruiting season. Brady and his head recruiter, Butch Pierre, had been criticized for offering me a scholarship.

In my mind, the Louisiana high school all-star game was the perfect opportunity to showcase myself as a player with the top competition in the state. I had been injured the day before the game to the point where I couldn't put much weight on my ankle the day of the game, but Coach Kenny Almond had put me in the starting line-up, and I didn't want to let anyone know how much my ankle hurt, fearing they might not let me play or would reduce my minutes. I prayed all day long that the sharp pain and the intense soreness would simply be taken away. Somehow I hid my limp for most of the day, playing it off when people would ask me why I was limping and whether I was okay. I got really loose and psyched myself to the point of not even believing that I had ever been hurt. When the ball was tossed up at game time, I literally didn't feel any more pain. To make a not-so-long story even shorter, I had twenty-one points as the game's leading scorer in only eighteen minutes and earned MVP honors as I helped lead the East team to victory over the West. Ironically, this was the first high school game that my parents had missed, having been stranded out of town and not being able to catch a flight back home in time to see the game. The further irony was that pictures of the game were nonexistent, and the video somehow malfunctioned! All I have to commemorate the game is the picture of me accepting the all-star game MVP plaque. Even though there were no videos or pictures, I had made my point; I belonged, and in my mind I had showed that I would be a contributor to the LSU team during my career there.

I remember being so excited about having played well in the all-star game. Two and a half months later when the LSU season was kicking off, I was excited about the promise of the new season. I realized that there were many people who thought that I would not only be a noncontributor during my first year at LSU, but that I was a wasted scholarship. During the introductions to the LSU team in October 1998, all of the media outlets in Baton Rouge—from the local newspaper, the *Advocate*, to LSU-specific sports papers like *Tiger Rag*—viewed me as a "legacy scholarship" and not as someone truly capable of contributing to the bottom line of any college program: wins. A local sportswriter, whom I've since become friends with, Lee Fienswog, wrote the introduction to the LSU team for the *Advocate* (the leading newspaper in Baton Rouge) in 1998. I remember, as he went through each new player, how in-depth his knowledge was of their stats at the high schools or junior colleges they had attended. He also knew what each would be expected to bring to the team that year. I was the last player on the list, and the only thing that was said about me was that my father had played at LSU from 1971 to 1974 and was the first African American to play basketball at LSU. That was it. Nothing was mentioned about my stellar high school numbers, which were actually higher than those of every other newcomer on the team, or the great high school all-star game performance where I had outshined all the rest of the best players in the state. I was SO mad when I read the article, and when I brought it to my dad, he just smiled (amused by how angry I was about it) and stated that it was my responsibility to force them to say something other than that. I used it as motivation. Interestingly enough, my mom's demeanor surrounding the types of situations I would deal with that helped strengthen my resolve to prove wrong those who doubted me was different than my dad's, which is to be expected. These people were, in her mind, making personal attacks on her baby! She was always more understanding and ready to be up in arms about the slights that would take place. Looking back, I believe that the significant challenges that my father probably dealt with during his college career helped strengthen the armor he wore and aided him in knowing how to coach me to deal with the extremely trivial (as compared with the situations he faced) and somewhat insignificant issues that I was dealing with.

Once I got to LSU and started my academic career, a similar situation arose when I made the decision to pursue and earn my undergraduate degree in three years. I was being coached by a couple of academic advisors that I might have been taking too heavy of a load of classes and that it might have been more beneficial for me to back off of that schedule and take it a little easier while getting started. The support system that the LSU Academic Center for Athletes provided was second to none in the country, but I was focused on doing some things that were not part of the normal progression and had not been done. With that in mind, I decided to follow my parents' advice and my own belief in myself and take the number of hours and the classes I felt I could handle, despite the precautionary recommendations of my advisors. After I performed well that first semester, I didn't have a challenge scheduling whatever I wanted during the rest of my time at LSU. They realized that they were dealing with someone unlike most of the students they had dealt with in the past.

WSTM LESSONS LEARNED

1. Identify the negative people who are around you and truly assess their value in your life. The best thing is to eliminate them from your circle, but if that's a significant challenge (for whatever reason), the next best thing is to use their criticism as fuel to become better.
2. There will unfortunately be people in several endeavors in your life who aren't in your corner. It would be nice if everyone wanted to see you do well and succeed at a high level, but it isn't reality. Realize that and deal with it.
3. Do your best to remain focused on the positive influences around you, no matter where they may come from.

Chapter 11

EVERYTHING HAPPENS FOR A REASON

*SUPERNATURAL—God does the SUPER
when we do the NATURAL,
and it works out for the betterment of all. —Anonymous*

*All a BIG SHOT is, is a SMALL SHOT that
just kept shooting. —Zig Ziglar*

I have always been a firm advocate that God has a greater purpose for all of our lives. That precept drives my belief that everything happens for a reason. I believe that we are in control of our destiny and that our decisions on a daily basis end up being the true determining factor in relation to our results and life circumstances—FREE WILL. With that said, I do believe that there is a little bit of luck involved, and certain things happen at certain points in our lives with a greater purpose than we usually can see at the point when they take place.

Going into my freshman year at LSU, from a basketball perspective, the coaching staff hadn't factored me into the equation as a contributor. My thoughts were different. John Brady had, in fact, talked to my father about attempting to convince me to redshirt. Redshirting would mean that I would not compete in games during my true freshman year, but would simply practice and possibly get an opportunity to travel with the team to get the experience of rival arenas. The idea of redshirting was not something I was in favor of, especially based on my belief that I could contribute during my first year on campus. John Brady and his staff had a guard-heavy team, especially after bringing in the recruiting class that I was a part of. Looking back on the situation, I think Coach Brady and his staff saw me as someone who would mature into a legitimately productive player during the later years of my career, as well as a quality guy in relation to locker-room morale, representing the team in the community, and bringing up the team's GPA. I saw my role differently. I knew I could do all of those things, but I also fully believed that I could be one of the best players on LSU's team very quickly.

Going into LSU after my high school career at University High, I was very well prepared from an academic perspective. That first summer I took six hours to get acclimated to the rigors of college courses. What I found out excited me and was a baseline of my academic success in college—it wasn't rigorous at all. I was fortunate, based on my academic success and the curriculum at University High School, to be more than ready to excel as a college student. After those first six hours, I went ahead and enrolled in nineteen hours that first semester. My academic advisors advised me that this was too many classes to take as a first-year student, especially as a student athlete. I ignored their advice, deciding that I would show them that I was not the normal student athlete. In my mind, I had taken five or six classes every semester that I was in school throughout my entire middle and high school years; what would be the difference in taking six classes while in college? I had talked to my parents, and both of them were supportive of me taking more classes, and my experience with gaining two A pluses during summer school boosted my confidence that I would be able to maintain a high level of success with my schoolwork. Also in the back of my mind was that fact that my mom had graduated from college in three and a half years while she worked part-time. I believed that I could do the same thing, but I had not mentioned it to anyone other than my parents.

For the first day of practice of the 1998–1999 year, Coach Brady had set up two-a-days, as well as for the following couple of days. It was a Saturday, and I was so excited when I pulled my practice jersey on that morning. I thought I had practiced well during the first practice and was eager about the second practice. The second practice was not really a practice at all but was LSU Fan Day, which would kick off an introduction of the team to LSU's fan base. Fan Day was the Saturday of a football home game and was set to start roughly four hours before game time. This of course meant that there were over fifty thousand people within the direct vicinity of Tiger Stadium and the Pete Maravich Assembly Center. There were about forty-five hundred people in the stands at Fan Day, but it looked like more because of the way they had set up only one side of the PMAC for seating, forcing everyone to sit in one area and making it look fuller. During our version of Midnight Madness, things started off with the player introductions. Then we got into two lines and started the common line layup drill. As the fans howled and cheered more loudly, some of the players started to show what they could do, dunking the ball and flying high. I especially remember one of the few seniors on the team, a guy I looked up to, Maurice Carter, jumping so high and dunking so hard that the crowd went wild. My juices were flowing too, and although I couldn't do the things Maurice could do—or many of the other guys, for that matter—I planted and took off to do a reverse dunk. The moment right after I planted, began moving under the rim, and twisted my body to dunk the ball, I felt a sharp pain in my right hip. Needless to say, I missed the dunk, but when I landed and gimped my way back to the other line, the pain, although not sharp, was still there. It was not only very hard for me to lift up my right leg, but it had also become hard to breathe. I moved to the opposite side of the court and lay down, and the trainer came over. I told him how I felt, and when he tried to pull me up, the pain was ridiculous. The determination was made that I needed to be moved to the training room across the street in Tiger Stadium so an X-ray could be done.

Although it was a short trip, it was definitely not one I was looking forward to. The trainer, Drew Shea, was someone I became close friends with, and he became an integral part of my life for the next few years. Drew, one of the managers for the team, and my dad helped me, with my mom following us, as we moved through the throng of people to the main training room. The eyes that I felt were looking at me with disgust, as if to say, "I told you he was a wasted scholarship." I've since learned that not only were those people probably not looking at me, but most of them could not care less about my basketball career. And because of where the LSU basketball program was at that point, many didn't even realize that there was a Fan Day going on in the PMAC.

As I lay on one of the training tables after they did an X-ray, my mother and father stood on either side of me. I looked up at both of them, saw how concerned they were, smiled inside, and said to myself, "There's nothing else I can do about this situation except look at the bright side!" At that moment, I looked at my mom and said, "Mom, didn't you graduate from Southern in three and a half years? She looked at me, somewhat perplexed, nodded, and said, "Yes." I quickly did the math in my head, remembering that I needed roughly 120 credit hours to graduate. My dad turned to look at me, awoken from his concerned state. I looked at both of them and said, "I'll just focus on my academics this year and get way ahead so I can graduate in three years. At first, both of my parents seemed somewhat stunned that I had changed the subject so quickly and turned the somewhat somber mood in the room into an interesting and more anticipatory excitement. They quickly recovered and joined in my focused energy toward the major academic undertaking.

That day I learned one of the major strengths that has aided me in experiencing success throughout my life, a strong point that I would have to use several more times during my career at LSU and throughout my business career: the bounce-back factor. The bounce-back factor refers to the amount of time it takes for someone to return to his or her normal—or in some cases, above-normal—level of mental energy or excitement after a seemingly tough blow, be it physical or mental. It is a true test of someone's mental toughness and emotional maturity. True champions always have a quick bounce-back factor and operate at the polar opposite end of the spectrum from the victim, who is constantly asking the age-old question that many victims ask: "Why me?"

The split-second decision I made while lying on that training table on the second floor of LSU's main training room helped shape the way I have dealt with tough circumstances and challenges throughout my life. As I look back on the difference it made in the outcome of my life, it's funny how, at nineteen, I had the mental wherewithal to come to the conclusion I did, make the decision I made, and quickly swing the pendulum of my feelings from pity and despair to excitement and enthusiasm in a matter of seconds, all while lying on the training table and waiting for the doctor and trainer to reenter the room. All of this happened only minutes after taking what, at my young age, may have been one of the toughest blows I had needed to deal with since I had wanted to play basketball at LSU and knew the opportunity even existed. I had worked my entire life up until that point to make that dream a reality, and during layup lines on the first day of practice, I was hurt to the point where I was out for the season. I had pulled a tendon out of place in my hip, and it would be several months before I could run normally again. You can't tell me that was not ordained timing! The incident was also foreshadowing for later points in my career. Later in life, once I had gotten into business, I had the pleasure of meeting and learning from Jim Winner, who wrote a book called *The Split-Second Choice*. In Winner's book, he talks about how big of a difference attitude makes in our ability to succeed. My grandfather, Collis Temple Sr., always told me, "Your attitude will determine your altitude!" Jim's book is about the decision-making process all of us experience along the attitudinal pathways of life. It helps readers recognize the critical points in our lives, careers, projects, and relationships. That Saturday afternoon in October of 1998 was a critical point, and I didn't even realize it. Without any prior formal coaching from Jim Winner, and without having read *The Split-Second Choice*, I navigated my way through the attitudinal phases I would learn to see in others and coach them through. I moved from having a negative mentality to shifting my thoughts toward a positive goal and focus. That shift in thinking has made an astounding difference in my life.

I came back toward the latter part of the season and was able to practice and travel with the team. It was a great experience that helped me a great deal. Many times in practice, I played the role of the leading scorer on the scout team that we were going up against in the next game. Assistant coaches Kermit Davis and Donnie Tyndall would give me the confidence that my time was coming, and that I just needed to stay ready, by giving me these assignments and privately pumping me up throughout the year. The opportunity to practice later that season was great, and the definitive decision to redshirt was huge in my development, especially considering that I got to LSU as a six-foot-five, 185-pound eighteen-year-old, and when I actually started my on-court career there, I was a nearly six-foot-seven, 205-pound twenty-year-old with a lot of confidence and belief in my ability.

Based on that decision that I made on that Saturday afternoon on the training table, I ended up graduating in three years with an undergraduate degree in general business administration. That was something I was proud to have accomplished, but completing my degree in three years and still having two years of remaining eligibility got my wheels turning. Thinking back to my grandfather's challenges in attempting to attend LSU in the early 1950s, I shifted my focus to taking advantage of the scholarship that I had earned as an athlete and having the university pay for me to get my master's degree. I applied and was accepted into LSU's Masters of Business Administration (MBA) program. During my first semester in the MBA program, I had some great teachers and met some phenomenal people, but I quickly realized that the MBA program was churning out corporate employees versus practically savvy businesspeople. I had learned it from an athletic perspective, but that was the first time that I truly thought, "Practical application is always much more effective when compared with theory." Although many of my professors were well-accomplished instructors, and some of them had even experienced some success in business, the majority were speaking from a position of theory and not practical experience. I realized, like Josh Kaufman talks about in his book *The First 20 Hours*, that you learn significantly more when you're forced into practical application of a subject rather than the theory and technical side of it. That applies in EVERY area of life. I decided to shift gears because, as I explained it at the time, "I don't plan on being a corporate robot. I'm going to be in business for myself anyway." I ended up finishing my master's degree in sports management that next summer in a year and a half, after completing my junior year on the court and with a year of eligibility left. That was an even bigger thrill than completing my undergraduate degree in three years, and it was an accomplishment that I dedicated to Collis B. Temple Sr.

My last year of eligibility at LSU I spent pursuing a PhD in educational leadership, or ELRC. That wasn't because I planned on becoming a principal or a professor, but because I said, "Why not?" I was always more efficient and effective as a student when I was busy, engaged in doing something, and working toward accomplishing something. After enrolling in the program, I was told by the sports information director for basketball, Kent Lowe, that I was seemingly the first collegiate athlete to have completed an undergraduate degree and master's degree and start working on a PhD all during the years of eligibility in Division I college sports. I was excited about that once I heard it, but it was not the reason that I had originally started the pursuit of the degree. The original mind-set revolved around a desire to remain engaged, involved, and active in something that I thought was extremely interesting.

Seeing the impact that getting hurt on the first day of practice during warm-ups had on the trajectory of my college career is crazy, considering everything that happened as a result of the injury. Had I not gotten hurt that day, I would have fought the redshirt and not completely turned my focus to finishing school early, and things may very well have ended a lot differently. It became apparent to me quite quickly after getting hurt that everything happens for a reason, and most times that reason isn't very clear right away, but becomes clearer as we move forward. As long as we control what we can and don't worry about trying to control what is out of our control, things usually work out as they should.

WSTM LESSONS LEARNED

1. Know your ROLE and know your WORTH, and work on increasing both of them based on your WORK!

2. Focus on controlling what you can and don't worry about the things that you cannot control. Think about all the things that you CAN control that you are not maximizing right now. Focus on making things better for yourself, your family, your team, your community, and so forth based on that focused effort.

Chapter 12

READY FOR THE BIG TIME?

Success is inevitable if you do the right
things long enough. —Art Williams

Your RESULTS are a by-product of
your ROUTINE. —Anonymous

Many people show up, but they don't show up to
do what's necessary to move up! —Bill Whittle

After redshirting through a first year that was not one of the banner years for the Fighting Tigers of LSU, things were looking up for the program, and I was extremely excited about my role in the resurgence of a program that had seen better days. During my redshirt year, we were 14–15. Maurice Carter, Jabari Smith, and Stromile Swift were bright spots that year, but the team never really pulled everything together. Going into my redshirt freshman year, LSU, with the help of assistant coach and head recruiter Butch Pierre, had again garnered another great recruiting crop by rankings and standards. Several of the people from my first year had left, including several guards who were incoming freshman with me but had played that first year and had made the decision to transfer. I was excited about that, but not because of lack of competition; I just thought it would give me more of a shot to be seen. I was determined to be a major contributor to the team, and I actually thought I could start, which anyone else around the program would have said was preposterous, including the coaching staff.

Even though several guys left, one of the crown jewels of the new recruiting class was a six-foot-three junior college shooting guard named Lamont Roland, who had earned the high honors of JUCO player of the year the season before, averaging over twenty-five points a game during his sophomore season. Another had already become a legend in some circles of high school basketball in Louisiana, having scored seventy points in a high school game. Torris Bright was a strong, quick, extremely confident, six-foot-four, two-hundred-pound point guard from Slidell High. Those two were immediately penciled in as the starting backcourt for the 1999–2000 season. Then came Brian Beshara, the six-foot-eight, tough, sharp-shooting combo forward, who actually played small forward based on the lineup. Next was the guy many didn't expect to stay in college too much longer, the ultra-athletic six-foot-nine Stromile Swift who, with a year under his belt, had grown into his body and was more ready than ever to wreak havoc on the rest of the SEC. Rounding out the starting lineup was Jabari Smith, the ridiculously skilled six-foot-eleven center.

Coming off the bench that year was my longtime friend and freshman roommate Jermaine Williams, who had become a favorite with the coaches his freshman year because of his versatility, unselfishness, and tough defense. Also off the bench that year was a newcomer and true freshman, and one of the highest and most powerful jumpers off two feet I have ever played with, Ronald Dupree. Dupree was basically the same height as me and was not as skilled from a perimeter perspective, but based on his toughness and athleticism, he was able to play power forward. There were even times that year when he played small forward with certain lineups. Rounding out the bench players expected to contribute was six-foot-eight sophomore power forward/center Brad Bridgewater, who had come in with Jermaine, Stromile, and me the year before. I completed the nine-man rotation as the back-up point guard and two guard. We really did have a strong and versatile team that year, and I was ready.

At the beginning of the 1999–2000 season, we were thought to be a talented team among circles around the SEC, but outside of the SEC, we weren't talked about very much. We weren't ranked nationally and weren't even thought to be among the contenders for the SEC title. During the exhibition season and the first few games of the season, we were beating teams by forty-plus points a game. For the third game of the season, we had a tournament in Honolulu, Hawaii. There were several solid teams in the tournament, and we were excited about the opportunity to show what we could do as a team. We played well during the tournament and won it, putting ourselves on the map as a team. I played a total of twenty-five minutes during the three games we played in the tournament. Looking back on it, as a guy not expected to play a huge role, that wasn't bad, but in my mind at the time, I felt that I was a better point guard than the freshman phenom, Torris Bright. I was probably the ONLY person who thought that, but in my mind, I was right. I had nothing against Torris; I just believed that I had a higher basketball IQ and that I could do a better job of running the team if given the chance. When flying back from Hawaii, I remember being dead set on transferring and leaving the school that I had always wanted to play at, LSU. I was ready to sign my papers and ask for a release. That was until we got home, and my dad talked me out of that way of thinking, letting me know that it was a long season and that we were only five games into the season. As I think back on the situation, it was the first time that I could remember losing my cool that bad and feeling as mad and frustrated as I did. I felt that I was outworking everyone on the team and was still not receiving a fair shot from Coach Brady.

Coach John Brady was a very interesting character, and he definitely played a role in helping me become the man that I am today. I still call him on his birthday to wish him happy birthday, and I call him on Father's

Day and wish him well on those days as well. I can honestly say that had you told me during my career at LSU that I would be doing that one day, I wouldn't have believed you, but I'm glad that I've grown to the point as a man where I can do these things. I say that because it was my belief during most of my time at LSU that Coach Brady was intimidated by my intelligence and the fact that I didn't need basketball as a "way out," and therefore I didn't necessarily need him. Coach Brady seemed to equate a kid's tough upbringing with his toughness on the court, and although I had far from a tough upbringing, there have been few guys I have played with who matched my mental toughness on or off of the court. I had a very militant mentality overall and was quick to speak up and let my opinion be known. I was never disrespectful, but I was outspoken. If you ask him today, he would probably tell you that I was one of the hardest workers on my individual game, if not the hardest worker, he ever coached, but I also had an opinion and I wasn't afraid to let it be known. I had been taught to respect the position of coach, but I also had very strong opinions about my ability. I never had an entitlement mind-set in thinking that I was owed anything, but I remember thinking that I was not being given a fair shot early on. It's funny, because even though he had given me a scholarship, early in my career I saw Coach Brady as being one of the people whom I had to prove wrong and show that I was someone who would be a major contributor to our team's success. This was something I would wrestle with him on early into my sophomore season.

Six games into the SEC schedule, we were 3–3, which wasn't great, but we had already gotten signature wins over top-twenty-five ranked Fresno State and top-ten-ranked Oklahoma State. Stromile Swift was really starting to get noticed based on his high-flying antics and ridiculous athleticism, as well as his numbers, and our team was starting to be recognized as a pretty well-rounded bunch. We were headed into a defining game for our team that year, playing the number-one-ranked University of Arizona Wildcats on national television. Arizona had three future NBA players (as did we), and the two guys who didn't end up playing in the NBA were actually thought of at the time as two of the best players on their team. Their starting point guard, Jason Gardner, was first-team All-American that year. They came into the PMAC with a 17–3 record, and we were 15–3. It was expected to be a great and highly contested matchup. We ran them out of the gym, beating them in every phase of the game and coming away with a convincing 86–60 victory to let the college basketball world know we were going to be something special that year. Stromile had a monster game, with twenty-nine points, nine rebounds, four blocks, three steals, and two assists, and he even stepped behind the three-point line to knock down a trey. It was a coming-out party for me as well. Torris, saddled with foul trouble, only played for seventeen minutes. The matchup between him and Jason Gardner was one of the main storylines of the game, but in his absence, I stepped in and played twenty-three minutes. My stat line was far from stellar: I scored six points, grabbed three rebounds, and dished out one assist to Stromile on a beautiful alley-oop from half court. I also made a nice move in the half-court offense that made Jason Gardner, considered by many to be the best point guard in the country, fall down. More important than the numbers, though, according to the television announcers, was the poise with which I played, ran the team, and played with such confidence against the best team in the nation. It wasn't a surprise to me at all, but it was nice to be recognized for it. Beating Arizona was one of the highlights of the entire season, and it was definitely one of the high points in my season. I played more minutes in that game than in any other game that season.

Although we had a letdown the next game, going to Mississippi State and losing by two, dropping to 3–4 in SEC play, we rebounded strongly to run the table the rest of the way in the SEC, winning nine straight and finishing the SEC season 12–4 and with a 25–4 regular season record going into the SEC tournament in Atlanta, Georgia, as SEC Western Division champions. Our first game in the SEC tournament was against the three-way SEC Eastern Division champs, Vanderbilt, which had the leading scorer in the conference and co-player of the year, along with Stromile, Dan Langhi. Langhi was a six-foot-ten small forward who could really shoot the ball well and was a great college player with a nice all-around game.

The guys we had coming off the bench played an extremely integral role in our team's success, and by the last quarter of the season, going into postseason play, we had caught our stride. Ronald Dupree, Jermaine Williams, Brad Bridgewater, and I were the four guys off the bench who completed the team's nine-man rotation. There were times that year where Ronald, Jermaine, and I really made the difference in the outcomes of games. More than any other time during the season, other than the Arizona game, I had worked my way into a main role coming off the bench going into the postseason. During our practice and shoot-around at the SEC tournament in the Georgia Dome, I felt great, and despite the sometimes prevalent challenges of depth perception that some shooters have when shooting and playing in a domed facility like the Georgia Dome, I had no such challenges. When the game versus Vanderbilt kicked off, I was the first guy off the bench, and I came in ready and confident. The game went back and forth, and at halftime, we were up. I had gone two for three in the first half, hitting one midrange bank shot off the backboard and a three pointer, while also missing a three pointer. I had already exceeded my average of under four points a game. I was the first player off the bench in the second half. Vanderbilt, realizing that they could not stay with us man to man, had gone to a matchup zone defense, and in the second half, I torched them, going five for five from the three-point range to finish the game seven for eight from the field and six for seven from behind the arc, finishing with twenty points in as many minutes. We won the game and moved on to the next round against the Arkansas Razorbacks, a team we had beaten twice during the regular season, but that was fighting for its own NCAA berth. The Razorbacks would not allow us to complete the trifecta on them that year, beating us by two in a great game. I actually didn't score as much but made a very positive impact for our team and played well. Their great freshman, Joe Johnson, played well and was a little too much for us to get by for a third time. We went on to earn a berth in the

NCAA Sweet Sixteen and lost to a defensive-minded Wisconsin team that went on to the Final Four before losing. I finished that year with averages of slightly over four points per game and slightly under two rebounds and assists per game.

The takeaways from that year were plentiful, but mainly I realized that I could be a contributor on a team where I wasn't the best player. It was a great learning experience in being a team player and playing a role to the best of my ability. I also had the opportunity to test my resolve around what I had been taught early on from my dad, that "you can't quit anything in the middle of a season, no matter how much you dislike it!" I truly wanted to quit on the LSU team five games into my freshman year after the Hawaii trip, but I didn't, thanks in large part to my dad's corrective conversations.

Another point that I think is very pertinent to mention is a specific situation that took place during that season, earlier in the year, when things got a little testy in practice. I always prided myself on being a respectable person and an all-around nice guy as well as an extremely hard worker and competitor on the court. In my mind there was not a conflict between being a respectable person and a fierce competitor, but that's not the way that many guys saw it. Lamont Roland, coming in from a Junior College (JUCO) and having a somewhat rough persona, seemed to think that he could mentally get to me, and he tried to, as we say, "punk" me during practice one day. We had already had a summer of playing against each other, and the beginning of the season was under way. I was somewhat frustrated by my lack of playing time early in the season, but dealt with it like I had dealt with anything else when it came to frustration in basketball: Get in the gym more. During a rebounding drill where I was doing what I always did and going all out like it was the national championship, he looked at me while we were waiting our turn to go in and told me that I needed to cool off, and that if I didn't, he would "deal with me." Any athlete knows the mind game that goes with this set of circumstances. If I "cooled off" and backed down based on him telling me to, it was a mental battle that I had lost that could have further-reaching effects. I also prided myself on never losing the mental battles. In my mind that was my proving ground, if ever there was one. That was where I made up for what I may not have possessed athletically. When our turn resumed in the drill, Lamont, Torris, and I were up. The coach threw the ball off of the glass toward Torris, and Lamont didn't even look to rebound it; he just lunged at me elbow first. What ensued probably helped me more than anything I did on the court in gaining respect from many of my teammates. We got in an all-out fistfight. Coach Brady jumped in, and because of the mental state I was in, he got hit with one of my punches as well. (In thinking back, I don't remember, but I wouldn't be surprised if I had intentionally hit him.) Making a not-so-long story shorter, after the fight, Lamont had to be escorted off the court by the trainer and go to the training room, and wasn't able to continue practice that day. I never left the court, continued practice, and had to be calmed down by several of my teammates and some of the coaching staff. I basically let Lamont know as he was being taken off the floor by the trainer that he had definitely mistaken me for someone who wouldn't fight back and was an easy win just because I was a nice guy. (I didn't say it quite that politically correctly, though.) A few weeks later, it got back to me that Lamont had told some people that he really had thought that I wouldn't fight back and that he was thoroughly surprised by what had happened. Not only did we have a better relationship after that happened, but he treated me with an entirely different level of respect. To me, that's how it works with almost all of the challenges that we face in life. If we cower and back down from them, they will overtake us, but if we "buck up" and face them head on, more than willing to fight for what we believe in, they'll back down and allow us to achieve whatever it is that we want. I've often heard my mentor in business, Bill Whittle, say, "Life will give you whatever you're willing to take, or whatever you're willing to TAKE! If you allow life to beat you down, it will; but if you stand up to life, it's basically a punk and will give you whatever you want!"

A third major lesson from that redshirt freshman year was one that I've seemed to learn over and over again under different circumstances:

Hard work pays off. I had put a lot of work in that went unseen, other than the normal recognition and average game that season. The Arizona game proved I belonged, but the Vanderbilt game showed that I might have what it took to be a lead contributor when the opportunity presented itself. The idea of doing what's necessary to be ready when opportunities present themselves was something that I was familiar with. Many times when people complain about not being given opportunities, it may be a valid complaint, but the main problem, I believe, is that when they finally get those opportunities, they are not prepared and don't perform admirably. I had always prided myself on being a hard worker and taking advantage of any opportunity that presented itself as soon as it presented itself! The Arizona and Vanderbilt games my freshman year did enough in my own mind to bolster my confidence for me to go to work at a level only rivaled by that of my junior year in high school, when I knew that it was do or die to make an impression on the college scouts. That first year playing, I made very clear to myself that I was not only ready and could compete, but that I belonged and would definitely be a force to be reckoned with. That's what I saw in my mind, but that wasn't exactly what everyone else saw. There were a few more "proving ground" types of situations that I would have to face right around the corner.

WSTM LESSONS LEARNED

1. Don't bail out on any situation you've truly committed to without letting it play itself out. Don't run from the process!
2. Remember that success is inevitable if you do the RIGHT things LONG ENOUGH. Ask yourself, "Have I done the right things, and have I done them for long enough?"
3. Never back down from your resolve, your belief in yourself, and your purpose.

Chapter 13

TAKING THE LEAD: LEADING AND BRANDING MYSELF AT LSU

*To be great, you'd better have a vendetta
with mediocrity! —Collis Temple III*

*Failure will embrace you, but you've got to
chase success down! —Anonymous*

*If opportunity doesn't knock, build
a door! —Carlos Gonzales*

Although the 2000–2001 basketball season was the worst of my basketball career from a win–loss perspective, it was one of the best school years of my life in terms of character development, learning to bounce back, keeping my head up despite challenging circumstances, and branding myself as a student athlete, team leader, campus leader, and an all-around person at LSU.

My redshirt sophomore year was a great year for many different reasons. I began really getting involved more in campus life in terms of extracurricular activities outside of basketball. I participated in student government, running for sergeant at arms, which I figured wasn't something that would prohibit me from continuing with my break-neck graduation pace, as well as basketball. I also was named the student athlete representative for the basketball team and the president of the Student Athlete Advisory Board/Council for all LSU athletes. I represented LSU, among all the other SEC schools, at the SEC home office. That was a great position that allowed me to stretch out and experience leadership on a higher level. It was also great to work with Mike Mallet and the Shaquille O'Neal Life Skills Program at LSU. This program sought out those athletes who were interested in volunteering and playing a bigger role in the community through the abundant service opportunities that existed. I had been made aware of the need to give back in the community by speaking to kids and spending time volunteering in as many ways as I could early on in my life because it was a way of life for my parents. I had been volunteering my time since I was in high school. I didn't even think of it as volunteering, but as just part of what I did and how I lived based on seeing my parents and the constant help and assistance they gave in the community. Because I spoke to kids so often in group settings, from opportunities in student government as early as sixth grade to speaking with younger kids when I was in high school about what it took to excel in high school as a student athlete, I had done it with regularity, and it was really nothing new. I also was a volunteer coach for the league I had grown up playing in, the House League at the Sports Academy. These things were all just ways of life and added to my appreciation of how blessed and fortunate I was to have grown up in the situation that I did. I was actually named LSU's student athlete volunteer of the year in 2000, 2001, and 2002. These were great honors because the award program began in 2000, and for me to be the first recipient was huge in my eyes. My thought process was that the things I was doing were necessary anyway, and if they were going to give an award for it, so be it. I never did any of the volunteering for recognition; many times I didn't even report when I went and addressed a school, talked to a church group, or went and visited a kid in the hospital. In addition, I didn't think it was really a fair fight in the first place. Baton Rouge was where I had spent my entire life. I loved the city and planned on living there even after I was fortunate enough to play professionally, and I was in favor of doing anything I could do to enhance people's quality of life in Baton Rouge.

From a basketball perspective, going into that summer of 2000, I was extremely encouraged by the way things had finished up for our team and also for me personally as a player the previous season. I also already had eighty-plus credit hours knocked out, and my plan to graduate in three years was right on schedule. I was extremely excited and ready to truly take LSU and the SEC by storm on the court. During the 2000 NBA draft, Stromile Swift was taken as the second player picked, and Jabari Smith went as the forty-fifth pick of the draft in the second round. With the departure of those two guys, there was an immediate need for the emergence of not only guys who could fill the void on the court, but also who could lead. It was not that either of them were the most vocal leaders, especially Stromile, but they led in their own way, mainly by their play. I was definitely up for the challenge of filling the leadership void, but it wouldn't be an easy transition.

Every four years, many Division I teams are given the opportunity to take a trip abroad to play against international talent. The reason this is a big deal is because the NCAA only allows teams to practice during certain times, and chances for coaches to get with their teams and have real game-time practice opportunities are a commodity. Before the 2000–2001 season, our LSU squad was fortunate to take a trip to Italy, with the chance to play several games against some of their professional-level teams. I came in with high expectations for my play and the trip, but the trip didn't live up to my own expectations. Part of the reason was because although Coach Brady and the rest of the staff had me down as a definite contributor, they hadn't quite figured that I would be playing as major of a role as I pictured myself playing. On returning from Italy, I realized that the main people who I needed to make sure knew that I had what it took to be given the reigns of the team were the coaching staff. Convincing the coaching staff probably seems like an obvious thing, but I truly thought that I had made enough of an impression based on playing well above their low expectations the year before.

That season we were still in the midst of NCAA sanctions on scholarship restrictions, just like the season before, but due to the loss of our two big men anchoring the defense and offense, we had a very different playing style based on our personnel. On top of the limited scholarships that year, Brad Bridgewater had an anterior cruciate ligament (ACL) injury, and he factored in as being our probable starting center. During the first SEC game of the season, the third starting guard, Lamont Roland, tore his ACL. It was as interesting of a season as I've been a part of. We started the year off well enough, 9–1, with our only loss on the road to a top-ten-ranked Arizona team that was focused on avenging the blowout it had received at the PMAC the year before. We played great team ball and were leading with eight minutes left in the contest, before Gilbert Arenas went bonkers in the last eight minutes and hit four threes, sparking his team to a run to finish the game that eventually saw us on the short end by thirteen points at the game's end. The following article from that season was written right before the start of the SEC season:

Rising Son
By Joey Papania
LSU Sports Information (January 6, 2000)
It was no surprise. Head coach John Brady needed to compensate for some major losses entering the 2000–2001 season. Jabari Smith finished his collegiate eligibility and entered the NBA draft. Stromile Swift left LSU early and was selected as the second overall pick in the 2000 NBA draft. And Brad Bridgewater, the Tigers' projected starting center, suffered a season-ending knee injury prior to the start of the 2000–2001 season.

The losses accounted for almost 40 percent of last season's points and rebounds, and the Tigers lost 134 out of the total &

180 blocked shots from the 1999–2000 season. It was no surprise that LSU would have to look elsewhere to fill the void.

Enter Collis Temple, III. The sophomore guard has provided an unexpected lift and has become a consistent scoring threat in this season's guard-oriented offense. But this new role was never a surprise for Temple. "I came in expecting to have to be a scorer, to shoot the ball more, to shoot at a high percentage and to shoot well at the free throw line," Temple said. "I'm really happy with the role that I am playing right now. It is similar to the role I played in high school. I was a scoring threat in high school."

The 6'6" guard has proven his scoring ability so far this season. He has seen action in all 10 of the Tigers' games this year and has started in all but one. He has also scored in double figures in every game with the exception of the Dec. 20 match-up against Arizona, the Tigers' only loss.

Temple's current 15.7 points per game average ranks him second on the team and seventh in the SEC. More impressive has been his accuracy from the field. He is currently shooting 52 percent from the field and 38 percent from beyond the arc, both stats landing him in the SEC's top 10 in each category.

His numbers have marked a dramatic turnaround from last year's four points per game average. Temple has already made 13 more field goals (50) and scored 26 more points (157) this season than he did in 33 games last year. "My role has changed a lot since last year, but I'm still approaching practice and games the same way I always have," he said. "I think I have adapted to that role well, and I have really enjoyed stepping up to the plate and becoming a major contributor this year."

One of his biggest contributions, especially in Brady's system, has been his production from the free throw line. Temple has helped the Tigers make 166 free throws so far this season, eight more than LSU opponents have attempted, a philosophy Brady feels is critical to the success of any basketball team. Earlier this season, Temple accumulated a streak of 19 straight made free throws. During that stretch, he went three straight games without missing a free throw (9–9 vs. Norfolk State, 2–2 vs. Houston, 5–5 vs. Texas Southern). He is currently leading the team with an 82.7 percent effort from the charity stripe.

Although the sophomore has taken tremendous strides from a year ago, he still feels his game needs improvement. "I don't think I am rebounding the ball as well as I should be, I need to get my rebounds up to about six or seven a game," Temple admitted. "I have accepted the role as a rebounder, I'm going to go to the boards whenever I can and try to get as many rebounds as I can. In high school, rebounding as a guard was my strength."

At 6'6," Temple has a height advantage on almost every guard he will match-up against. In order to compete in the SEC, the Tigers will have to rely heavily on Temple to hit the boards. He is one of the tallest active members on this year's team.

LSU will also have to rely on Temple's leadership abilities. He is one of the most vocal members on this young Tiger team. "I've always thought of myself as a leader," Temple said. "Even when I was a red shirt freshman, I always approached practice as some-one who gets the guys going."

LSU tore through its early non-conference schedule to the tune of a 9–1 start entering conference play. LSU should expect to be the target of revenge in the almost every SEC match-up where the Tigers amassed a 12–4 record a year ago and captured the 2000 SEC regular season title.

LSU handed every team in the SEC Western Division at least one loss on their road to the Sweet 16 in 1999–2000. In the two games that LSU faced Alabama last year, the Tigers outscored the Crimson Tide 171–126, including a 33-point victory at Alabama. But Temple does not think the fact that the Tigers will be tar-geted will deter the team or him from achieving this year's goals.

"I think we are a team that has a legitimate shot at winning 18 to 20 games and making the NCAA Tournament this year," said Temple. "Personally, I think I have a chance at being named All-SEC if I can continue to improve the level I am playing at. I think I also have a shot at making the SEC Academic Honor Roll this year and maybe even Academic All-American.

So far, so good for the young Baton Rouge product. The Tigers' biggest test begins now with the start of the SEC season. If the Tigers hope to continue the early success of this season, it will be because of the hard work and dedication of players like Collis Temple, III.

It's funny to look back at that article now, knowing the season that we ended up having that year, but it's a great indication of how confident I was in what we could accomplish. After the legitimately strong start, we proceeded to lose the first six SEC games, all by less than nine points, before beating in-state opponent Centenary by forty points. The next SEC game was at Mississippi State, and I had the best offensive game of my college career until that point, leading our team to victory: twenty-seven points, six rebounds, and four assists, shooting ten for eighteen from the field in thirty-five minutes. It was the type of offensive game that I believed I was capable of on a regular basis; unfortunately for both me and the team, it wasn't the type of game I delivered enough that year, because we didn't win another SEC game for more ten games, beating Ole Miss in Baton Rouge by only one point in overtime. The next game was in Thompson Boiling Arena in Knoxville, Tennessee, home of the Tennessee Volunteers. I had my best offensive performance of my college career in that game, scoring thirty points, shooting eleven for sixteen from the field, and hitting six three pointers along with six rebounds and four assists. Ronald Dupree, who was the foundation of the entire season and simply a warrior, also had a game above his normal seventeen-point average, at twenty-three, but it still wasn't enough, as we lost 78–71. That year we played 75 percent of our games with only six scholarship players, but we were in most of the games until the last five minutes, when we simply ran out of gas.

Going into the SEC tournament with a 2–14 SEC record, I remember thinking, "Hey, we still have a chance at the NCAA tournament! We could RUN the table and win the SEC tournament!" You're probably thinking that I was just being positive, and obviously I was, but I actually believed that we had an outside chance to do it. We had almost been in EVERY game that season with the exception of three, when our lack of depth would catch up with us toward each game's end. Despite the horrendous record that year, we didn't really lose much of the fan base, which really taught me a lesson that season. I had never lost like that on any team I had been on, but because we played so hard, were in almost every game and gave it all we had. The fans, announcers, and everyone who seemed to be involved respected us and truly rooted for us. Also, coming off of my best game of the season, I was on somewhat of a high. As a competitor, when you do something well, many times the belief is that you can do it again on a regular basis. I was no different, and I felt that if we could somehow turn things up as a team, maybe, just maybe, we could pull everything together. That didn't happen in the tournament, but what did happen was that we played the NCAA tournament–bound Georgia Bulldogs and pulled off the upset that kept them out of the tournament that year, playing the role of spoiler before falling in the next game to Arkansas. I had played a horrible game for thirty-four minutes against Georgia in the first game of the SEC tournament, but in the last twenty-two seconds, I scored five points (hitting a thirty-foot three pointer and knocking down two clutch free throws), got a steal, and defensively held in check their leading scorer for us to seal the win and spoil Georgia's NCAA tournament hopes.

That year was such a character-building season for so many reasons, but on top of that, it taught me how to not only remain positive personally, but how to remain positive while leading a team of people under challenging circumstances. Before each game, I remember thinking, "This will be the game we catch a break, and the ball bounces our way." I've never been someone who believed in luck. Our 2000–2001 team worked extremely hard and just didn't have enough firepower. Throughout the challenges, I emerged as a vocal leader who could be counted on to not only perform to the best of my ability on the floor, but also to lead from every perspective that was necessary—from working hard in practice and in the weight room, to being an example of how to carry myself as a student athlete in the classroom, on campus, and in the community in general. I embraced the role of captain my sophomore year before I was officially named the team captain the following year.

From a leadership perspective, that year I learned how to lead a group of my peers through a less-than-ideal situation and do everything I could to see the best in it. It was a lesson in continuing to work hard toward the accomplishment of a goal, despite everything not working in our favor along the way. I'm not a huge proponent of the old adage that "losing builds character," but I must admit that the 2000–2001 season was a year that played a pivotal role in my development as a leader and as a man. Having to face and speak to the media after loss after loss, and having to face family, friends, acquaintances, and just the normal fans around town, made my character stronger, and I was definitely more humble as a result of that season.

After the 2000–2001 redshirt sophomore year on the basketball court, I walked across the stage and received my undergraduate degree in business administration after three years of college. I was excited for a lot of reasons, the main one being that I had set a goal under the tough circumstances of getting hurt two and a half years earlier, and I had followed through and accomplished something that very few students accomplish, much less student athletes. I was proud to have been disciplined enough to follow through and do it. It enhanced my already very robust self-image and self-confidence. I truly felt like I could accomplish anything that I put my mind to and worked toward.

I started thinking that having an MBA while I was in the NBA would be a unique plus that I could probably take advantage of. I started the MBA program at LSU, and it was a great and challenging program. I learned a great deal during that first semester; however, I did realize that the program's primary objective seemed to be getting its students jobs in corporate America versus the practical application of truly enhancing the students' knowledge and putting them in a more aware position to open their own businesses and excel as masters in the business world, which was what I was more focused on doing. I always knew I wanted to go into business for myself, whether it was with my parents or something on my own. At no point did I have it in my mind that I was going to go to work at a normal nine-to-five job—not that there's anything wrong with that, it just wasn't what I saw for myself.

After the first semester, I settled on finishing up my master's degree in sports management, and fortunately most of the classes I had taken in the MBA program in the first semester carried over. I ended up finishing the master's degree in sports management the summer after my redshirt junior year, my fourth year of college. Earning my second degree was something that I was extremely proud of, but not for the reason that many people would be. First of all, I had taken full advantage of being on scholarship at LSU and earned two degrees in four years and a summer. Second, I really liked the idea of representing for the student athletes and somewhat disproving many of the dumb stereotypes that were out there about student athletes and their inability to compete in the classroom. The last reason I was proud about the rare accomplishment was because, in my mind, it somehow was retribution for what had happened fifty years earlier with my grandfather, Collis Sr., not being allowed to attend LSU and earn a master's degree from the flagship university in the state that he grew up in.

WSTM LESSONS LEARNED

1. Always have high expectations for yourself! If you don't, it is extremely unlikely that anyone else will.
2. Give back whenever and wherever you can. It makes a HUGE difference.
3. Remember that many great leaders emerge during challenging times. Stay focused and positive all the time, and especially when less-than-ideal situations arise.

Chapter 14

FLYING HIGH AND GETTING GROUNDED: THE BOUNCE-BACK FACTOR

Talent is God-given; be humble. Fame
is man-given; be thankful.
Conceit is self-given; be careful. —Anonymous

The stronger your character is, the greater
your growth potential. —John Maxwell

Following a tough redshirt sophomore campaign on the floor from our team's perspective, but one in which I had experienced a personal breakout year, along with my fellow sophomore teammate Ronald Dupree, I was excited about what we could accomplish our junior year. Adding to the excitement for me was the fact that I had earned my undergraduate degree and was working toward a master's degree. Going into my junior year, I was stronger than I had ever been, bench-pressing nearly three hundred pounds and squatting over five hundred pounds. I was more athletic than I had ever been in my life and healthier than ever. Pickup games that summer were such a breeze. I had played basketball competitively for fifteen years and had never felt more in control of my body, more fluid in my movement, or more natural in the rhythm of my jump shot, my ability to handle the ball, or anything else on the court, for that matter. At six feet seven inches tall and 210 pounds, I remember feeling—and in almost every case, actually being—stronger than any perimeter player I was facing that summer. I was, as to be expected, quicker, faster, and much more fluid than any inside player I went up against. Our team was looking as ready as I was personally, with our core group of juniors in place—Torris Bright, Ronald Dupree, Brad Bridgewater, and me—to go along with senior Jermaine Williams. Obviously, by this point in the book, one of the things you have ascertained is that based on the baseline and foundation laid by my parents, the one thing I really never lacked was CONFIDENCE! Going into this season, I would honestly say that I was borderline COCKY when it came to where I was as a player. In the early part of the season and practice, it was extremely obvious who had not only emerged as the vocal leader and captain, but who was easily the best all-around player on the floor for our team. We started the season off strong, just like the year before, with me and Ronald Dupree leading the charge. We jumped on the competition early on, going 8–1 in the first nine games. Through those first nine games, I was leading the SEC in scoring and rebounding, averaging 19.5 points and nine rebounds. Ronald was second to me in the league in both scoring and rebounding, at eighteen points and 8.5 rebounds per game. The following article sums up my strong start that season:

Temple Named SEC Player of the Week
Published: December 2, 2001
BATON ROUGE—LSU junior guard/forward Collis Temple III was named the SEC Player of the Week on Monday for his two back-to-back 20-plus point games against Towson (Nov. 28) and Northwestern State (Dec. 2). Against Towson, Temple made 10-of-12 (83.3 percent) shots, totaling 24 points, seven rebounds, five steals and two assists. Temple also scored 24 points versus

Northwestern State on 7-of-14 shooting, including 4-of-6 from three-point range. He also totaled 13 rebounds, four assists and two steals. He averaged 24.0 points, 10.0 rebounds, 3.0 assists and 3.5 steals for the week. He also shot 17-of-64 (.654) from the field and was 6-of-9 (66.7) from behind the arc in both games. This marks Temple's first SEC Player of the Week honor.

I remember the wheels turning in my mind ten games into the season, already with degree in hand and playing lights out; I started thinking about how amazing it would be to be in a position only five months from that point to be able to legitimately leave early and go to the NBA. It was only a thought in my mind, but the reality was that I was putting up great numbers, and after that year, I would not only have gotten my undergraduate degree, but would also be close to finishing my master's degree. I started thinking, "What else would there be left to do?" If I was in a position where I had averaged between nineteen and twenty points per game and eight to ten rebounds per game and threw in four-plus assists a game, as a versatile six-foot-seven, 210-pound guard, I would be a commodity. Add on to that the fact that I had been great in the community and had a clean résumé and record, and I actually began to think that I would be an NBA general manager's dream! About that time I had even started showing up on the early draft boards and similar lists where players around the country were ranked by people who, I've since found out, really don't know anything different from the average sports talk radio personality.

Despite all the thoughts floating around in my head about the possibilities of me accomplishing my ultimate dream of playing in the NBA earlier than expected, the most pressing things in my mind remained that season, our LSU team's success, and the continued growth of my ability to lead, along with the continued growth of the relationship with the people of my hometown, Baton Rouge. It honestly seems unusual that a college athlete would be thinking this way beyond his or her sport, but that's really how my mind worked. The reality, however, was that the thoughts, although rightfully ambitious, slightly took my eye off of the focus at hand, just slightly enough. I had started reading my own press clippings. The success DEFINITELY didn't dampen my work ethic or the burning competitive fire that I had inside me; if anything it proved to me why I needed to turn things up. I really learned that staying the course, keeping things in perspective, and remaining focused are the best ways to handle high levels of success. It was a lesson that has served me well to this day.

Have you ever begun experiencing the success you'd desired in a particular field and allowed the success to slightly dull the laser focus that it took to get you there? I cannot honestly say that that was my situation, because I remained an ultra-focused person, but I do believe that had I not started paying attention to that outside stuff, things may have ended up a little differently.

Two games after being named SEC Player of the Week, we were playing McNeese State for another in-state rivalry game. I had come off of a nice game before that against the University of Louisiana–Lafayette. In the first three minutes of the game, I stole the ball and was all alone on a break-away dunk. I planted, planning to do an acrobatic dunk, and my ankle gave out. I had sprained it badly, and didn't return for that game or the next one. Although I returned for the following game and hobbled to lead our team to a victory over Houston in a 20-point effort, I was playing at about 75 percent, and it went down from there. I didn't know it at the time, but that was the beginning of the end of my basketball career.

One of the most frustrating things to deal with after being injured was knowing the level that I had played at during the beginning of the season and knowing the level that I dropped to as a result of trying to play on a bad ankle before I just hung it up for the season and got surgery. I can honestly say that I was MISERABLE! I went to school, went home, and started rehab as soon as I could after surgery. Of course, hindsight is 20/20, and looking back, before attempting to return to the court after one game out, I should have remained out for the length of time that truly allowed my ankle to fully recover, but that was extremely hard for me just based on my competitive spirit and my desire to play. I did things to get back on the court that, looking back, I should not have done, and that I would not allow my kids to do if they were in the same situation—taking shots to mask the pain, and things like that. I was never forced to do anything; if anything, I was pushing the issue. After ten to twelve games of totally subpar play due to my injury, I shut it down and got surgery. Once the late Dr. Larry Ferrachi got a look at the MRI, we discovered how bad the injury was, and that it was worse than we had originally thought. I had almost entirely torn a tendon in my ankle. Unfortunately for me, it was one of the tendons that controlled the stability of my ankle. To this day, I can step on a pebble and sprain my ankle. I still remember what Dr. Ferrachi told me as we discussed the options of the surgery: "Collis, this fix may only last for two to three years, but it could last longer depending on the wear and tear." Anything that would get me back to the court, I was ready for!

Unfortunately, I was a veteran when it came to rehabbing from injuries, but the severity of this injury, especially in a sport like basketball with the type of injury it was, made things tougher. I knew the mentality that it took to approach rehab like a warrior ready for battle. I was going to make sure that I did everything that was necessary to experience a full recovery. Many times in life when people are faced with challenging circumstances and situations, the way they respond to those situations is oftentimes more important that the situation itself. I had dealt with the bounce-back factor, from an injury perspective, earlier in my career on the first day of practice my freshman year, but the difference then was that I hadn't yet begun accomplishing anything of significance during my college career. When I was injured during my junior year, I had started the ascent of my college basketball career. I was finally poised to start experiencing some of the fruits of my labor on a national scene after nearly fifteen years of putting in work. Not to discount the mental fortitude I displayed while lying on the training table that Saturday in October of 1998 as a true freshman, but mentally bouncing back from an injury during that redshirt junior year meant more than it did during my true freshman year. Although I presented a good show on the outside, at that point in my life, dealing with that injury was easily one of the top three toughest things that I had dealt with. (Considering that to be extremely accurate, I would say that I had an extremely blessed life—and you would probably agree!) I went through a mini-depression in realizing that not only would I have to rehabilitate extremely hard to get back to the point I had been at physically, but even more than that, I would have to work that much harder to regain the mental hold on Coach John Brady. He had finally admitted that I was in fact his best player, after several years of him seemingly thinking of me as a nice guy. He looked at me as someone who could bring the GPA on the team up and be a nice role player who would graduate from LSU and have a fulfilling, but very mediocre, basketball career; to him, I was someone who didn't add much on the court, but did not lose much either. Coach Brady seemed to not want to admit that I had broken through his glass ceiling of belief in me as simply a nice role player.

The team went on that year to the National Invitational Tournament (NIT), with the efforts of Ronald Dupree and Torris Bright and the emergence of the freshman who had taken my place after I got injured, Antonio Hudson. I was proud of Antonio because I felt like he was somewhat of a little brother of mine. The summer before his first year, we had spent time together, with me mentoring him about on-court and off-court things. After his emergence as a main cog in the team's success that first year, I was well aware that the stage was set for us to be an even better team the following year. But it would be that much tougher for me to regain my position as "king of the hill," which was totally okay with me.

My final year of eligibility at LSU was the 2002–2003 season. Based on the way I had played during my career, some would have thought that I was OWED a starting spot after the way my junior year ended in injury. There's no such thing as being OWED anything! We need to get that straight. If I had come in my freshman year and outplayed someone, my mentality was that I should get the spot. It is truly a situation of "what have you done for me lately," and that doesn't negate the value of loyalty, but it's the coach's job to put the team in the best possible situation to win. I fully understood that and was not under any delusion that if things were the other way around, I wouldn't expect the exact same treatment. We were bringing back almost everyone from the previous year and had several strong newcomers my last season. We had talented depth at every position. I was extremely hopeful about our goals as a team and had a well-founded and complete expectation that we would go far in the NCAA tournament.

My senior season started off well for us as a team, even though I could realize that I was not in the same physical space that I had been, coming off of ankle surgery a few months earlier. Whereas the year before I was a terror for opposing teams as a rebounding guard, I was not rebounding as strongly as I had, partially because of the better personnel that we had and partially because of where I was physically. We had picked up the Junior College Player of the Year in the form of an undersized center named Jamie Lloreda, who was a relentless rebounder. In addition, we had the ever-present pogo stick that was Ronald Dupree as well as Brad Bridgewater and, coming off the bench early in the season, the very talented—even if he was unstable at times—Shawnson Johnson. The third game of the season, after beating a few warm-up teams by thirty-plus points, we traveled to Reliant Stadium in Houston to take on Texas A&M, which had a solid, top-twenty-five-ranked team and a high-scoring duo. One member of this duo, Bernard King, was from Louisiana and was in the process of breaking the school's scoring record. The other, Antoine Wright, would be a lottery pick in the NBA draft a year later. We were ready for the nationally televised game, and although we didn't play great, we did go toe to toe with them before falling short and losing 79–77. I played pretty well offensively, leading our team and scoring nineteen points, but it wasn't quite enough. The next four games, we beat the teams we played by an average of twenty-four points, and it was good that several different players got opportunities to show their skills. Then, on December 21, 2002, the number-one-ranked team in the nation came into the PMAC to play us on ESPN, with Dan Shulman and Dick Vitale commentating the game. The following article was written prior to that game:

Article from LSUsports.net (December 17, 2002)

Sleep is not often high on Collis Temple's list of priorities. When you're a Division I college basketball player who has earned bachelor's and master's degrees in just over four years, every hour of every day is precious in working to attain your goals.

"I have a motto, 'You can't get ahead staying in the bed,'" said Temple, who will receive his master's degree in sports administration Friday at LSU's commencement ceremonies. "I get up at 4:45 every morning and do the things most people don't do in order to be successful. I plan to enter a doctoral program next semester, and my goal is to be an NBA player with a doctoral degree."

When Temple arrived on the LSU campus in the fall of 1998, few would have taken his ambitious aspirations seriously. He was not one of the Tigers' more highly touted recruits, though he did enjoy a stellar career at University High in Baton Rouge. Characterized as a role player when he began his career—Temple, whose father, Collis Jr., was an all-SEC player at LSU in the early '70s—exceeded expectations and developed into a full-time scoring and rebounding threat.

While emerging as a force on the floor, Temple also thrived in the classroom, and the 6–7 guard earned a bachelor's degree in only three years, receiving his general business diploma in July 2001.

And, just over a year later, Temple, a three-time member of the SEC Academic Honor Roll, holds a master's degree with an opportunity to earn a PhD.

Temple and the LSU Tigers will be on the court of the Maravich Assembly Center Saturday night at 7 p.m. against the No. 1 college basketball team in America, Arizona. The game will be televised on ESPN2 with Dan Shulman and Dick Vitale announcing. Tickets are available for $10 at the LSU Athletic Ticket Office (225-578-2184) and on the Internet at www.LSUsports.net. One fan will have the chance at halftime to make a half-court shot and win $10,000 in the Eagle 98.1 FM Shot Contest.

The demands of school and sports would consume most student-athletes, yet Temple is also a frequent participant in community-service projects in local schools and hospitals.

"The way I look at it, God has given me great gifts, and it's only right to take advantage of those by helping other people," Temple, said. "The fact of the matter is, athletes are role models, college or pro. We need to do all we can do to be nice role models, to be good role models, to be role models parents would like their kids to emulate."

When speaking to young people, Temple espouses a philosophy that has served him well.

"The thing I stress is everybody is not going to be an NBA basketball player, everybody is not going to be an NFL football player, everybody is not going to be Bill Gates and make $50 million a day," he explained. "But, everybody can be successful in his or her own way. I tell students that being successful doesn't necessarily mean you're a millionaire and you're making a lot of money. It's you being able to deal with obstacles in a positive manner. You set goals, and things will turn out well for you."

Temple also is in his second year as president of LSU's Student-Athlete Advisory Board, which acts as a support group when an athlete encounters a difficult obstacle.

"There are times when an athlete may not feel comfortable telling a coach about a problem he or she might have," Temple said. "So, they may come to us, and we can help them deal with the problem as a group. We're all coming from the same body, instead of one person just out there by themselves."

As a redshirt freshman, Temple helped the 1999–2000 Tigers, led by NBA draft selections Stromile Swift and Jabari Smith, win 28 games, capture the SEC title and advance to the NCAA Sweet

16. Now, as a seasoned veteran, Temple sees similarities between that championship club and LSU's 2002–03 unit.

"I think this is a team that is still coming together, still finding our identity, still meshing," Temple said. "We are extremely talented and deep; we don't have the No. 2 pick in the draft (Swift), but from top to bottom, we're more talented than the 2000 team that won all those games. If we can come together as a collective unit, we can accomplish the same types of things that team accomplished."

As Collis Temple's LSU playing career concludes this season, he can reflect on a college experience that, while never relaxing, was extremely rewarding.

"When I first came in, most people doubted me, but I think I have evolved into a player who, because of my size and because of my basketball knowledge, has a chance to play at the next level," he said. "But, I'm also a person who doesn't need the NBA to be successful. I think that's the most important thing that I have accomplished since I've been at LSU."

We marched into the PMAC excited and ready and came out with a great 67–66 win in front of a crowd of ten thousand LSU fans, many of whom stormed the court after the game. It was the signature win of the season for that team, and it gave us a record of 8–1 for the season. I remember being happy for our team and our major accomplishment, but I had not played well, grabbing six rebounds but only scoring four points on a largely ineffective two out of seven shots and playing for only twenty minutes. While the rest of my teammates went out and enjoyed the shine of having won such a big game, I went home that night. I couldn't sleep because of the thoughts of my poor play. At around 11:30 p.m., I got out of the bed, went back to the gym, and worked myself out and shot for another two hours, more as self-punishment for not having performed on such a large stage the way I believed I should have to make a push for my goals of becoming a legitimate NBA prospect. My answer for almost everything was simply WORK HARDER.

We had an extremely interesting season my senior year, going 2–7 to start off the SEC season in the doldrums. In addition to us not playing well as a team, I was in a shooting slump for much of the beginning of the SEC season. Unfortunately (or fortunately, depending on how you look at it) the only way I knew, and have ever known, to get out of a slump of any kind was to WORK my way out of it. That forced me to overwork my body, as the doctors said, and not get enough rest, which aided in me getting sick halfway through the SEC season. Interestingly enough, it became a defining moment in my career and in that season for us. We had a game at home against Vanderbilt in the middle of the week, on a Wednesday. During our normal film session on Sunday afternoon, Coach Brady and I got into a rare argument in which he told me that if I continued to shoot the ball and miss, he would pull me. I say *rare* because it was never my mode of operation to have any type of adversarial relationship with any coach I had, but it seemed like Coach Brady would "try" me at every opportunity. His exact words that day were, "Fine, keep shooting—but the first time you miss, I'm pulling you!" I was so hot after that film session, but for the next two days I had flu symptoms so bad that I didn't even attend class or practice. The team's trainer, my friend Drew Shea, brought me the medicine I needed to my house. On Wednesday I was feeling better, but not 100 percent. I went to shoot around, and Coach Brady and I didn't speak. I was penciled in as the starter at shooting guard just like I had been for the previous two and a half years. That night in the first half, I took out the frustration of my shooting slump, of getting injured the year before at the height of my career, and with Coach Brady on Vanderbilt. We blew them out of the gym, and I went five for six from the three-point range and six for seven from the field in the first half, only missing one shot, to score seventeen first-half points. At halftime I made the smart-aleck comment to Coach Brady that I didn't want to come out of the game, so I just didn't miss. He liked that cocky attitude; he was weird like that. After the game, Coach took credit for getting me to rest, which enabled me to shoot my way out of the slump, and said he had full confidence in me and that my biggest problem was that I was my own worst critic and overworked myself physically. There may have been a little bit of truth to a few of those statements. After the Vanderbilt game, we went on a tear and won six of our last seven regular-season games, finishing the SEC at 8–8 as we made our late-season push for the NCAA tournament. We won two games in the SEC tournament before losing in the championship game to the Mississippi State team, which was already bound for the NCAA tournament. In the process of making that push, we also had several games where we set records and played some of the best games of all-around TEAM basketball that I've ever been a part of in my basketball career. Based on that push, we went into the NCAA tournament as one of the hottest teams in the country.

That senior season ended with a very disappointing loss in the first round of the NCAA tournament to Purdue, where we just flat out didn't play well. Just like that, the LSU basketball career that I had dreamed of having as an eight-, nine-, and ten-year-old was over. It was time to move on to the next phase of my dream, playing in the NBA.

WSTM LESSONS LEARNED

1. How quickly do you "bounce back" from seemingly negative situations and circumstances? Really work on the mental game of quick recovery and finding the positive in every situation.

2. We are NEVER owed anything. One of the quickest ways to a definite demise is feeling entitled to something you haven't earned!

3. Hold yourself to high standards. Use a system of rewards and punishments to continue to grow and improve. When you perform well, reward yourself; when you don't perform to standards, punish yourself! This is a great way to build self-accountability.

4. Ask yourself, "Could I be accused of overworking myself?" Most people would say no if they were being honest. There are a multitude of people who lean toward too much leisure rather than overwork.

Chapter 15

I GOT MY SHOT!

Go confidently in the direction of your dreams.
Live the life you've imagined. —Henry David Thoreau

You imagine the image you want
of yourself. —Anonymous

I can remember the feeling of disappointment after the Purdue game, and yet also some anticipation of what was to come. I had wanted to play in the NBA since I was six years old, and unlike the phenoms who are able to make the jump from high school or after one or two years in college, I had gone the distance. I had experienced a little bit of that feeling of having a chance to do it the previous year before going down with an injury, but I was just as determined as ever despite not having a completely stand-out senior year.

I had, for all intents and purposes, already picked out the guy who I knew would represent me as an agent, so that wasn't an issue. The focus was creating interest, and without an invite to the college showcase camp, Portsmouth, or any opportunities to work out for any teams prior to the summer league, I was simply putting in work and doing what I knew best—working on my game for several hours a day, getting work in the weight room done, and doing everything to get in the best condition that I had ever been in. I went to Houston for several weeks to work out with John Lucas, the former NBA coach and a guy whose judgment NBA teams trusted. I had a great showing while working out with Lucas, but I was forced to cut my trip short due to reinjuring my ankle. That's how the next few months went: I was working hard, but was literally spending 50 percent of my time in the training room recovering, never truly 100 percent healthy. Despite those somewhat challenging circumstances, I continued to work and got my body to the point where I was stronger than I had ever been during that time, getting my bench press up to 330 pounds, which wasn't bad for a six-foot-seven guard with my build. For a short period of time, I even got the lift in my legs back that I had experienced during my junior year, but for the most part, it was a frustrating process.

The draft came and went without the miracle of my name being called based on me not having been asked by any teams to come and work out for them. I was only slightly disappointed, but not surprised at all. In my mind, it was just another opportunity to prove the doubters wrong and live up the high standards that I had always set for myself, despite setbacks and seemingly insurmountable obstacles.

My agent, Oscar Schoenfelt, had started the process of looking both in the United States and overseas for opportunities. That's when Joe Dumars, the general manager for the Detroit Pistons, called and offered me the opportunity to play with the Pistons during the summer league in Orlando, Florida. This was the first of two NBA summer leagues; the second one was in Las Vegas. That year's draft was a very deep one, with Lebron James being picked by the Cleveland Cavaliers, Dwayne Wade by the Miami Heat, and Carmelo Anthony by the Denver Nuggets. The first two guys were in the Orlando summer league with their respective teams, which made that league a spectacle in itself. I was so excited about the opportunity and anxious to prove to myself that I could in fact compete with these guys at the highest level of basketball. Although my agent had represented some significant players in the past, he hadn't had a player of any major relevance in a few years, and no team really owed him any favors, so I realized that the opportunity to play on the summer league team was based on my merit and ability as a player.

The Pistons had just come off of a good season in which they had fallen short in the playoffs and hired a new coach who was a staunch fundamentalist and one of the best coaches in the NBA, Larry Brown. Because it was his first season coaching the Pistons, Coach Brown, along with his entire staff, coached the summer league games. Also on that staff was Coach Mike Woodson, who became a head coach in the league. I was excited about the opportunity to play for a guy who I had watched coach greats like Reggie Miller. The reality was that Coach Brown loved fundamentally sound, hardworking guys who respected the game and didn't take the opportunity for granted. That was a perfect description of me.

When I first got to the summer league, I didn't know what to expect. Everything was taken care of—the room we stayed in and all the transportation. We were given so much per diem to eat with every day that I still had money in my bank account two and a half months later from the per diem we had been given for the week and half that we were in Orlando. I was also excited that my college teammate, Ronald Dupree, would be a teammate with me on Detroit's summer league team. Ronald and I had done battle together many times, and the opportunity to further our careers together at the next level was an extremely exciting potential future. Also on the team was an old foe from the SEC who already had one year of NBA experience under his belt, Tayshaun Prince. I was ready to show myself, and anyone else who cared, that I was definitely capable of playing and competing at the highest level of basketball in the world.

The first few practices were simple enough, and it was still such a surreal experience that I was this close to accomplishing my lifelong dream of playing professional basketball in the NBA. I remember going through the first couple of days of practice and realizing that I could not only compete with but outplay many of the guys in the summer league. By the end of the summer league, I had made a name for myself as a smart and versatile player who could not only play both guard spots but also small forward, and depending on the lineup, Coach Larry Brown even had me playing some power forward. There were several awards given after the summer league. I was named one of the top three shooters in the Orlando league that summer based on the clip at which I shot the ball from behind the arc being an impressive 64 percent.

After the summer league was over, I was extremely sure of my ability to play and compete at the NBA level. At the end of the league, Larry Brown had a quick conversation with me. He said, "Collis, you've definitely got what it takes to play in this league. Now, you won't be playing for the Pistons, because we've got two great players under contract that play the position you play in—Tayshaun Prince and Richard Hamilton—but keep at it, and stay with it." I had made enough of a splash in the league to be contacted by Chris Alpert of the National Basketball Developmental League (NBDL) with a midlevel contract offer to play in the NBA's minor league. I signed a contract with the league with an expectation that I would be able to get a call-up to the NBA within the first few months of playing. I remember the day that the paperwork for the contract came in and I signed it, realizing that although I wasn't in the league yet, I was one step away and was going to play professionally. I was training hard, getting stronger, and strengthening my all-around game. My agent, Oscar Shoenfelt, was also checking for opportunities overseas.

I was working out with a couple of different guys and playing pickup basketball with a group of guys who knew the game, making the games better and making it easier for me to really work on my game versus just running up and down the court. One of the guys, who was a speed and agility trainer and had played football at LSU and in the NFL, was a guy named Scott Holstein. I wasn't being trained by Scott, but he was playing pickup with us, and I got to know him pretty well in a relatively short period of time. Scott was a nice guy, and about five to six weeks into playing pickup a couple of times a week with him, he asked me after we'd finished a day of playing if I would come take some time and speak to some kids from his church, take pictures, and sign autographs for them. I immediately agreed that I would come on the following Saturday. When Saturday came, it was a hot day. The festivities for the event were outside, but it was a great experience, and I had a lot of fun spending time with the kids. After the event, Scott offered to pay me for my time, and I quickly declined. He then offered to take me to lunch the following week. I agreed to go to lunch with him that following Monday at noon, because other than working out all day, I had nothing else specifically going on. He mentioned that he'd probably have Bill Whittle come to lunch with us. I knew Mr. Whittle because he had played basketball with my dad at LSU, but I actually knew him more so based on his son, Blake, who was only a year older than my youngest brother, Garrett. Blake played AAU basketball during the summer, and Mr. Whittle coached his son's teams. Even though Garrett and Blake played at different age levels during the summer AAU season, every once in a while they would play against each other.

That Monday morning came, and I was in my normal routine of getting up before 6:00 a.m. and knocking out my morning weight workout at the LSU weight room in Tiger Stadium. After that I would run ten to fifteen stadiums, running up the bleachers. I had finished up a great weight-room workout and was running my stadiums when, on the way down the stairs after having run my seventh stadium, I took a lazy and tired misstep. My right ankle buckled under the pressure of my body weight. As I felt the ankle turn, I knew it was bad—it was my right ankle, the one that had already been surgically repaired, which only made matters worse. I was in pain, but at that moment, more than the pain of reinjuring my ankle and the imminent rehabilitation program that I knew would have to take place, I felt something that I was not very used to: the pain of UNCERTAINTY. I sat on the bleachers in Tiger Stadium, the only person sitting in the stadium, which at the time held over ninety-two thousand people, and started crying. I had just turned twenty-four years old the previous month, in September. Despite ALL the injuries I had dealt with and challenges I had experienced, this was the first time in my life since I was six years old that I experienced any doubt in the possibility that I might have a ten-year NBA career.

WSTM LESSONS LEARNED

1. If you had a goal that you didn't accomplish, could you honestly look in the mirror and say, "I truly did absolutely everything humanly possible that I could to make this happen"? If you can say that, but it didn't work out, you should not have any problem moving on—but if not, it will haunt you.
2. Be prepared to perform when opportunities present themselves!

Part III

THE TRANSITION TO THE REAL WORLD

Chapter 16

RE-RAILING MY DREAM: I FOUND IT!

Don't get comfortable where you are. There's something bigger, something better, something more rewarding in front of you. —Joel Osteen

Reinvent yourself and be more dedicated to your future than your past. —Anonymous

Since that Monday on October 20, 2003, I've always said that there have only been about six hours in my life from six years old to twenty-four years old that I wasn't 100 percent sure of what I was going to do and the path that I was going to take with my life. During the summer of 2003, my dad, although he was always extremely supportive, had started hinting, as the injuries and the time spent in the training room mounted, at not chasing the basketball dream past its time. His argument was that I had so much more to offer the world than just bouncing a basketball and could impact my community in so many significant ways. He was definitely not discouraging me from playing, but he was trying to get me to realize that I had several options, especially having done what I had done as a student athlete at LSU. I had established a name in my own right in the Louisiana community as a solid young man of intelligence, character, and integrity.

After I pulled myself as together as best I could under the circumstances, I limped down the stairs and into the training room. I can honestly say that the next few hours were a blur, but I basically spent some time in the training room before dejectedly returning to my home and taking a shower. I then retreated to my room for the next few hours, only talking to my younger brother, Elliott, who stuck his head in my room to ask what was up. I dryly replied, "It's over..." He asked what I was talking about, and I simply didn't reply, not wanting it to be true.

Other than God, I honestly don't know what prompted me to keep the appointment that I had with Scott for noon that day. I really didn't feel like leaving my house, my bed, or the pity party of uncertainty that I was in at that time, but fortunately for the rest of my life and the lives of countless others, I kept the appointment. I did not really have an idea of what was in store and how much that meeting would actually change my life.

I pulled on a brown velour sweat suit and left, heading for TJ Ribs restaurant, which was only five minutes from where I lived. As I limped and labored into the restaurant, I saw Scott and Mr. Whittle sitting at a table. Both rose to greet me. They were both sharply dressed, yet for me it was just a "payback" lunch, and although I felt underdressed, I didn't mind too much. I could tell that Mr. Whittle was in good shape, and although it had been a while since I had last seen him, we gave each other warm handshakes and greetings. We sat down, ordered, and just started talking. I let them know that I was pursuing my dream of playing professional basketball in the NBA and had experienced a challenging setback just a few hours earlier. Mr. Whittle started asking me questions, and after a few minutes, I started thinking to myself, "Is this guy interviewing me?"

I had actually always wanted to be a businessman. From a relatively young age, I innately understood the idea of creating my own FREEDOM and a great QUALITY OF LIFE by having control over my TIME and MONEY. As mentioned earlier, I had had conversations with my dad as early as eight years old in which I would ask him why people worked for him and my mom instead of going in business for themselves. I always knew I wanted to be in business for myself; I just didn't know what business it would be. I had worked in every area of my parents' nonprofit business, the Harmony Center Inc., from the accounting department to serving as a direct-care staff member in a couple of homes with residents. I admired what they did and the difference they were making. I realized that the jobs that they were creating for people were helping these people become productive, tax-paying members of society who led productive lives and could afford their cars and mortgages and build their families. That was a big deal to me, and I also remember the difference they were making for the clients of the facilities, when, in many cases, there weren't other places that would take these folks in and help them. I built relationships with some of the clients and with several of the staff. At one point they had over four hundred full- and part-time employees statewide. I had experienced firsthand the freedom that being a successful business owner could afford; I wanted to not only play professional basketball in the NBA, but also to build an empire in some business as well.

Slavery is no longer legal in the United States. It is no longer a regular practice to sell humans as chattel, yet despite the fact that people don't have chains and shackles keeping them locked into their current circumstances, people are still not free. That's because the things that limit their ability to TRULY be free are their limited or nonexistent control over the amount of money they are paid at a job or their limited control over their time and what they can do with it, based on the amount of hours that they are allowed or demanded to work at their jobs. True FREEDOM and QUALITY OF LIFE involve both TIME and MONEY, and thanks to my parents and the lifestyle they provided my brothers and me, I understood that.

About four weeks after the season was over during my last year at LSU, I was recruited into a company called Quixtar. I later found out that the company was a spin-off of Amway, the extremely successful network marketing company whose owners, among other things, own the Orlando Magic and whose name is on the arena that the Magic play in. For me, however, despite having several meetings at my home (the largest of which had twenty-five people at the house) and personally getting on auto ship for the first month, as well as getting a few other people to purchase some products, my first check was so small (less than ten dollars) that I didn't see the need to continue. In my mind, I was going to the NBA anyway.

That summer after my last year of eligibility, I also had begun inquiring about buying certain franchises, such as Smoothie King and Raising Cane's, as business opportunities. I planned to use the disposable income that I was expecting to earn as a professional athlete to generate more passive income. I had even gone to real estate school and gotten my license that summer to earn the commissions on the properties that I would buy as I started building my portfolio, as my parents had. That's actually how I was first introduced to the brokerage model of business— through real estate. I remember that after I had passed my test and was looking for a place to park my license, I asked the broker at a local real estate company how quickly he could help me move from being the agent to being the broker. He looked at me with a puzzled look and reminded me that such a move wouldn't be possible for at least two years—which I knew from just having passed the test—but even then, he didn't seem too excited about the prospect of training me to get my own real estate agency. I later realized that the primary reason he wasn't wildly excited about training me to build my own real estate agency and helping me become a broker was because that would, for all intents and purposes, mean that he would no longer override my business. I quite realistically would become more competition for him.

BUSINESS MODELS

Primerica is the company that has provided me with the platform to impact lives internationally and create a great lifestyle for myself and my family. Primerica serves as the largest independent financial services marketing organization in North America. The company has been in existence since 1977, and is a member of the New York Stock Exchange, with its NASDAQ symbol being PRI. The company has more than two million investment clients with nearly fifty billion dollars in assets under management. Primerica also has nearly four and a half million life insurance clients and pays three million dollars in claims on a daily basis. These astounding numbers have been achieved without the use of national television or radio advertising!

The Primerica business opportunity was presented to me by Bill Whittle, and I was not familiar with the company; I had, however, experienced, at least at some level, three of the great business models that exist in American business:

1. Brokerage model
2. Franchise model
3. Network marketing model

I realized that they all had pluses and minuses.

The brokerage model provides opportunities, for simply the cost of licensing in most cases, to get started primarily in some form of sales. For the most part, there is some level of mentoring for the agents by brokers who have a vested interest in the agents' success in the form of overriding income off of their sales. The brokers usually have the better quality of life based on freedom of time and money, but the agents eventually have the opportunity, if they desire to and work hard enough, to experience that same level of freedom and quality of life that the brokers enjoy. In the brokerage model I had experienced in the real estate industry, brokers had freedom of time because homes were being sold and bought whether they were the ones personally selling the homes or not, based on how many agents they had licensed and trained as a part of their brokerage. Therefore, they didn't have to be PRESENT to generate their income. They had the ability to make as much money as they wanted based solely on the amount of agents they were willing to recruit, train, and develop. The letdown of the brokerage model was that the brokers, in every case that I was aware of, were not incentivized to build other brokers and, in essence, create their own competition; therefore, they had to remain engaged in the process forever because, for the most part, the strongest agents would aspire to become brokers. I was exposed to the real estate model of the brokerage business, but it applies similarly to insurance and investment brokerages, both of which require state and federal licensure. Both the real estate and financial services industries are well respected and some of the oldest and most vetted industries in American business. They also control an extremely large part of commerce in the United States and have been around in one form or another for longer than the United States itself has existed.

The next model, the franchise model, is different in that it requires, in most cases, more capital. In my experience, in many cases the amount of capital was significant. The promise was that you were buying into a proven system and business model and that all you had to do was duplicate the already successful process. Raising Cane's was still in its infancy as a company and was just beginning to explore the concept of franchising, and I wasn't willing to be a fry cook for two years and learn the ins and outs of the chicken-finger business, primarily because I wasn't PASSIONATE about it. Smoothie King was another option in my mind because I loved what the franchise offered as a product, even if I wasn't PASSIONATE about marketing it. The truth in both of those cases was that even if I had been passionate about what those two companies did, I didn't have the money to pay the initial amount for a franchise anyway.

Entrepreneur magazine's "Top 10 Franchises of 2014" showed that the average range and cost of those top-ten franchises was between $634,170 and $2,296,433 to start up. That is not including operations cost past the first few months, and in many cases only includes initial startup. Couple that with the fact that 93 percent of businesses fail within their first five years of existence. Although a proven system is extremely valuable and seriously important, the cost to start is prohibitive for most people without access to significant capital resources.

Then there's the network marketing business model. It is a direct selling method in which independent agents serve as distributors of goods and services and are encouraged to build and manage their own sales forces by recruiting and training other independent agents. With this method, commission is earned on the agents' own sales revenue as well as on the sales revenue of the salesforce recruited by the agents and their recruits. Another common name for network marketing is multilevel marketing (MLM). It is a multibillion-dollar worldwide industry that distributes all different types of products and services. Usually the network marketing model offers the opportunity for those to go into business who may not have the capital resources to do so via other more traditional business models. The pros of network marketing are the low startup costs and, in the right situation, the continual self-improvement that is necessary for people to grow themselves into the people they need to become in order to truly be successful. Other positives are that, in most cases, there are no territorial restrictions on where recruiting can take place, which means unlimited success to the people willing to deal with the challenges associated with building their business.

As challenging of a situation as the 93 percent failure rate presents, think about having a looming debt that still has to be paid despite not having any revenue coming in from the now-defunct business. The fears associated with going into business are not phantoms but real challenges that even the most well-planned-out business may face. Entrepreneurs must be willing to deal with the realities of these challenges head-on in order to experience the success that they want and get to the proverbial light at the end of the tunnel.

Getting back to TJ Ribs on that twentieth day of October in 2003, we continued talking, and Mr. Whittle told me about the company he was associated with and owned an agency with. He explained what the company did and what it was about. I had ordered buffalo chicken tenders, but as the conversation continued, the thought of my food was further and further from my mind. He pulled out a presentation, and although I had an undergraduate degree in business and had gone through finance and economics courses, had a master's degree, and had even started working on a PhD in education, I didn't have any practical knowledge of what he was talking about. I had never heard of Primerica. As a single, twenty-four-year-old young man with no children, no mortgage, and no formal job at the time, I wasn't in the primary market of people on which Primerica focused its efforts in relation to its client base.

As Mr. Whittle talked and explained further about the company, I was blown away by the amount of information I didn't know about personal finance despite my degrees, as well as coming from a fairly well-to-do family. I immediately realized that if I didn't know these basic but extremely necessary and quintessential financial concepts, MOST people didn't know them! I had always wanted to be in business, and had just figured that I'd take over the nonprofit business that my parents had started. The two things that mattered the most in my mind were doing something that would make a real impact on people's lives and satisfying my desire to make a significant amount of money for the purpose of living the lifestyle that I wanted to live and provide for the family that I didn't even have yet. The impact that my parents' businesses were able to make on people was unbelievable, and they were able to do well financially as well, but the idea of generating $250,000-plus monthly in income without having to worry about being traded, hurt, cut, having the state or national government change programs, or HAVING to work based on the income being PASSIVE was very appealing. It wasn't because I didn't want to work, but I just didn't want to HAVE to work, and I was willing to pay whatever price was necessary for however long was necessary—as long as it was legal, moral, and ethical—to put something like that in place.

I was also blown away by the HYBRID business model of Primerica. Primerica had the best of all three of the business models that I understood the basics about:

Brokerage: Recruiting, training, licensing, and developing agents whom you can override.

Franchise: Helping people who have the desire, the work ethic, the stick-to-it-iveness, and the mental toughness to actually open their own agencies as Regional Vice Presidents (RVPs). Based on meeting certain criteria, they could actually own to the tune of a valuation of seven to ten times annual income.

Network marketing: Unlimited recruiting opportunity without territorial restrictions.

After hearing the entire presentation, I was actually sold that first day. It was amazing that I had just been hurt and had finally begun coming to the realization of there being a possibility, for the very first time in my life, that based on my physical situation, I may not be able to experience a ten-year NBA career. Despite that blow only hours earlier, I was totally and completely submerged in thoughts of success with this company that I had just heard the name of an hour and a half earlier. Mr. Whittle gave me several brochures, magazines, and other information and coolly ended our intriguing conversation with, "Take a look at the information, and give me a call in a few days if you're interested."

I learned something that day that I didn't truly realize until I had been in the business for about twelve months. WINNERS ARE CHASERS! I went home and immediately started tearing through all of the information I'd been given. I read EVERYTHING! I didn't browse or skim but devoured every piece of information that I had taken from the meeting. That night I could not sleep! I woke up at midnight, 3:00 a.m., and 5:00 a.m. I knew that was way too early to call Mr. Whittle, so I went back through some of the information until the clock turned to 7:00 a.m. Then I called him and, attempting to sound as smooth as possible, told him I had taken a look at the information and thought I might be interested. When he said we should set a time to get back together, I asked him what he was doing that day. We met later that day, and he explained the specifics of the process of building what could become MY business! I loved the idea of that, and when he let me know that most people earned their RVP promotion within eighteen to thirty-six months, I looked at him and told him I'd do it in half the time, nine months. After our meeting, I followed him to his office, signed up, and was full-time in the business. I still hadn't talked to my agent yet. That evening I spoke with my mom and dad. The advice from them as two successful businesspeople, from my mom first, was, "As long as you've got basketball out of your system, you'll be successful at whatever you decide you want to do!" And from my dad, "You'll help a lot of people, and you're working with a great company—a great guy in Bill Whittle—and you'll need a Brinks truck to carry all the money that you'll make. GO FOR IT!" I didn't need confirmation from anyone else, not that I was looking for it from them.

Too often I see people who are looking for validation from people who honestly shouldn't matter in their decision-making process. YOU don't need to ask anyone's permission for you to be successful! And WHY in the world would you ask ANY advice about business, money, or success from someone who has never experienced it or knows NOTHING about it? That mistake continues to and will always BAFFLE my mind. I often use this analogy: My mom is an amazing woman in so many ways and a phenomenal businesswoman. I would ask her advice about a lot of things, but if my car broke down on the side of the road, I wouldn't be calling her. "Why wouldn't I call her?" you ask. BECAUSE SHE'S NOT A MECHANIC, and as great at many other areas of life as she may be, FIXING CARS ISN'T ONE OF THEM. That's what I would need advice on at that moment. It's extremely important that we COMPARTMENTALIZE whom we get advice from in certain areas of our lives. We can have mentors for several areas in our lives—our spiritual life, our marriage, our parenting, our business endeavors, our relationships in general, and more. One surefire way to MAXIMIZE your life is to get advice from people who are great in a specific area that you'd like to be great in and practice what they suggest. Who says you can't be great in every area of your life? Why not?

MY FIRST TWO YEARS IN BUSINESS

I readily admit that my start in my business, despite my initial and genuine excitement and supportive parents, wasn't totally perfect. I dived headfirst into the business. I called my agent by the third day, Wednesday, and let him know that I was retiring. I called the NBDL administrators and asked to back out of my contract, which they allowed me to do. However, I was still facing interesting circumstances. After two weeks in, before the third day of a four-day state licensing class, I was summoned to my dad's house. He said, "Collis, I know you're excited about Primerica, and I think you're gonna do great at it, but I've got to let you know that an offer has been made for you to go to Italy and play. They're offering roughly two hundred thousand dollars, housing and car expenses paid for, as well as allowing you to rehab for as long as necessary. I'm not suggesting anything, but just letting you know what's on the table. It's obviously your choice, and I'll support whatever you do." I thought about it while sitting at the kitchen table in my dad's house. As hard as it was, I decided that I was doing what I was supposed to do and declined the offer before heading to licensing class. Ask yourself, "What would I have done?" I believed in the opportunity and the person coaching and mentoring me to be successful, but, much more important, I believed in MYSELF. If so many other people before me had been able to experience high levels of success, there was no way that I wouldn't experience great success. In my mind, if only one person had succeeded, the opportunity to do so existed.

Another reality of my first year in business was that I couldn't watch basketball on TV, because many of the guys whom I had played with, many of whom I had outplayed, were experiencing success. Although I was genuinely happy for them, it was hard to accept that I wasn't there as well. I fixed it in my mind that THIS was my sport now. As soon as I was starting to be able to deal with my decision, my college teammate and friend, Ronald, who had played with me on Detroit's summer league team, was called up to the Piston's team from the NBDL. In his NBA debut, he had exploded for eighteen points and seven rebounds off the bench with several ESPN highlight dunks! Seeing Ronald really made me question my decision, but after a few hours, I fixed my thought process. I refocused and was back at it.

During my first two years in business, I experienced a relatively significant amount of success. I worked hard enough, and based on that effort was blessed to come in contact with some amazing people. In helping them to achieve some of the things they wanted to accomplish, I accomplished a great deal. Those first two years went by really fast, even though they never really seemed like they were when I was going through the tough stuff. True to what I had told Mr. Whittle I would do, I moved quickly and efficiently through the qualification and promotion process. My first year in business, I earned $61,000, and within ten months from signing my paperwork and nine and a half months from my license date, I'd done enough to earn control of my own agency as what the company called an RVP. The second year in business, I earned $252,000 and exceeded the income that I had been promised to earn in Italy that first year, with nothing guaranteed further. The way I looked at it, with as many people in the company earning at least $100,000 a year, I figured that my success WAS guaranteed based on me doing what I was coached to do by someone who was already extremely successful doing it! January of 2005, thirteen months after getting licensed, was the first month I would earn over $20,000 in a month, and I didn't look back from there. I had proven my thesis that I could earn the income, create the lifestyle, and make the impact that I wanted with this company, and I was hungry for more. I was like a shark seeing blood in the water; I couldn't get enough. I had found it, my new sport, my new competitive proving ground, my new home! I was saving 70 percent of my income and was extremely excited, and my success in business was giving me the opportunity to experience that lifestyle that I had dreamed of, from the money to the fame and feelings of BEING SOMEBODY!

Those first two years in business set me up to explode my income and my business in general. In addition to making money, my already confident persona in front of a crowd speaking was improved and polished significantly. I really started learning how to connect with groups of people and improved my ability to talk to people and connect with them one on one and face to face. Another small but significant shift was in my true understanding of how powerful actually writing my goals down EVERY DAY, several times a day, was. I had always been a goal setter and had written my goals down. For the most part, I even looked at them daily, but accepting the coaching from Bill Whittle to write them down several times every day took me to an entirely different level. Ironically, writing my goals down twice a day and keeping up with my daily planner was the thing that I was the slowest to adopt as a habit, yet it's been one of the major reasons for my success. This process enhanced the already strong three common denominators that I already had as baseline beliefs surrounding my success.

We've covered the validity in my life of writing down daily goals and affirmations earlier, in chapter 5. The baseline of belief I placed in the value of writing down my goals came from that earlier point in my life, but that idea was turbo-charged with the information I gained and learned from Bill Whittle. The ideas that Mr. Whittle was teaching me were re-iterated through self-help and success coaches like Brian Tracy and his *GOALS* audio training. The power of writing goals down is amazing, and it's significantly enhanced the more you do it! To further illustrate the power of writing down my goals and affirmations, a book I read by Henriette Klauser, *Write It Down, Make It Happen*, talks about the power of the reticular activating system, or RAS. I had heard about the RAS from Bill Whittle, and it intrigued me. Klauser contends that "putting it on paper alerts the part of your brain known as the reticular activating system to join you in the play." During those first two years I fully discovered the power of writing my goals down first thing in the morning and last thing at night. As a giant in the area of mental toughness training, Steve Siebold says in his book *177 Mental Toughness Secrets of the World Class*, "When the goals are set, champions put mental blinders on and move forward with dogged persistence and ferocious tenacity. World-class performers create such an intense level of concentration to overcome challenges and achieve goals that it is the last thing they think about before they fall asleep, and the first thing that hits them when they wake up." That's the approach that I took with my daily planner. In another of my favorite books, *The Answer* by John Assaraf and Murray Smith, the authors mention that, "The more clarity you create around your business in every aspect, from its largest objectives to the particulars of your everyday actions, the more you harness the mind-boggling power of the quantum field to do your bidding and bring that idea into reality." All of these are extremely powerful examples of the application of the already aforementioned power of focus, as well as the use of the daily planner in the success process that became habit for me.

As a result of reading and listening to a myriad of books and audio programs in an intense effort to speed up my personal growth and enhance my already robust belief in myself, I threw myself into anything that gave me insight about how I could accelerate my success. I was not interested in shortcuts, but I was interested in lasting improvements and changes that could help create fast success. I let people know that I truly had no boundaries on what I was willing to do, as long as it was legal, moral, and ethical.

During these first two years I also grew a great deal as a leader. I remember thinking that I was a good leader prior to being in business, based on the fact that I outworked people and had garnered the respect of my teammates and coaches, but what I realized was that great leaders are able to raise the levels of their teammates, enabling the entire team to play at an entirely different level of success. I began to realize that everyone didn't want it like me, and that instead of challenging them with asking why, I would do much better by asking, "What is it that you want out of this?" Then I would help them get it, and if they were interested, I would help them graduate to a higher level of desire, which in turn would lead to a higher level of success for the person committed to accomplishment of his or her goal. I truly believed I could do anything after making the successful transition from being an accomplished student athlete in college and aspiring professional athlete to the world of business. I was breaking records along the way simply based on applying the same success principles I had applied to every other area that I had succeeded in during my life.

Those first twenty-four months were a whirlwind that only got faster after that. I was beginning to receive invitations to speak all over the country and talk about what I was able to accomplish in a short period of time. I also became a featured fixture in several company publications, including a national publication, the magazine *Success from Home*. During the company's international convention in Atlanta in June of 2005, I spoke on the main stage in front of over thirty-five thousand people. I remembered my mentor, Bill Whittle, telling me early on, while we were on our way to our first speaking engagement together, that people would ask to take pictures with me and may want my autograph. I didn't believe it. In my mind, I couldn't see people treating someone in business that way. I was completely wrong, and I discovered the controlled celebrity status that can be achieved when you've done the work that most people haven't and have experienced a level of success that most people haven't seen. It really isn't a lot different from athletes or entertainers. I've never been the guy who wanted anyone's autograph. For some reason, that wasn't me. The only jerseys that I ever wore other than my own were a Michael Jordan jersey and an Anfernee Hardaway jersey, because he was a big point guard like I wanted to be. I had relationships with the likes of Shaquille O'Neal and Mamoud Abdul-Rauf, and I never wanted their autographs while they were at LSU. My mentality was that I was capable of working just as hard as them, and therefore I could have what they had. I learned later the role that God-given ability played in the equation, and that in some cases it created a separation. What was interesting to me was that in this business, the God-given differences didn't exist; it all came down to the mental game, which in my mind meant a totally level playing field. THIS WAS IT!

When I speak of re-railing my dream, I'm talking about the belief that I had something to fight for again, something to truly believe in and be totally sold out to and excited about! Prior to business it had been my basketball career, but when I was injured and came to the realization that I wasn't going to experience a ten-year NBA career, success in the realm of business became my total intent. I've often told people that the only way that I could walk away from basketball was because I truly had the belief that I had done everything humanly possible to make that dream become a reality. I walked away knowing that I had given it my all. Because of that truth in my mind, I was able to mentally transition to my business and give it my total focus. I've noticed that guys who are successful as athletes often have a tough time transitioning successfully into the work world after athletics because of their inability to transfer the focus, work ethic, and coachability that were hallmarks of their success as an athlete. That was a strength that aided me in experiencing success quickly.

WSTM LESSONS LEARNED

1. If freedom is defined as your quality of life and is determined by the control you have of your time and money, ask yourself, "Am I truly free?" If not, what are you going to do about it?
2. Remember to not take advice in any specific area from someone who is not experiencing success in that area of life. Ask yourself, "Whom am I asking for advice?" Also ask, "Am I asking for advice in an area where that person has real expertise?"
3. Believe in yourself and your ability completely enough to bet everything on it. That's real commitment to yourself.

Chapter 17

MENTORSHIP

*Remember that mentor leadership is
all about serving. Jesus said,
"For even the Son of Man came not to be
served but to serve others and to give his
life as a ransom for many" (Mark 10:45). —Tony Dungy*

*What I've found about it is that there are some
folks you can talk to until you're blue in
the face—they're never going to get it and
they're never going to change. But every once
in a while, you'll run into someone who is eager
to listen, and willing to try new things.
Those are the people we need to reach. We have
a responsibility as parents, older people,
teachers, people in the neighborhood
to recognize that. —Tyler Perry*

T he definition of *mentor* is a "wise and trusted counselor or teacher," and with that being the simple definition, I've actually had MANY mentors! I've had people I had close relationships with as mentors, and

I've had people who mentored me from afar, some of whom never knew that they were serving as a mentor of mine. I've even had mentors who no longer were alive during the period of time that I was able to benefit from their knowledge and incredible insight because I was gaining the knowledge from a book about them. Anyone open to learning and hungry for knowledge will always be able to find mentors. All the resources and opportunities to do anything and everything we want to are all around us, if we're willing to reach out for them. One of my closest mentors, Bill Whittle, taught me, "God puts the grapes within your reach, not in your hands!" One of my strongest and best traits is that I've always been willing to reach for and put the effort into finding out what I needed to in order to succeed at the level that I wanted to, and I was never afraid to ask for advice or assistance.

Mentorship is an extremely important aspect of growth, which is the only way to ascend to the next level in any capacity. I still have yet to meet the successful person who has done it totally on his or her own, without any valuable insight from an outside source, a mentor. We've all heard that there's no such thing as a self-made man, and as I've learned, if you're able to accomplish your goal alone and without assistance from anyone in any capacity, what you're accomplishing can't be that big or significant. As I mentioned, mentorship is an important part of growth, and all growth demands change. Having a quality mentor who can assist you in making the necessary and possibly painful changes that must take place in order for you to accomplish your goals in whatever area you're looking to improve in is why mentors exist. Most of the time, the person or people you choose to mentor you have accomplished what you are looking to do, and if they're willing to spend time with you to impart knowledge and wisdom, it is definitely a must to not waste the time they've invested in you by not applying the information.

Other than the two people I covered extensively in the beginning of this book, my parents, Collis Temple Jr. and Soundra Temple Johnson, there have been others with whom I built close personal relationships and from whom I gained knowledge, confidence, and inspiration in shaping my thought process and mentality. My parents, specifically my father, were very intentional about the people they allowed me to be influenced by. I can point to so many different people, such as Gerald Furr, the legendary high school coach at University High School, who would sometimes let me run drills with the varsity when I was a puny but confident sixth grader. He helped boost my confidence and belief in what I could do as an athlete. I can point to Mailon "Choo Choo" Brooks, who, as one of the coaches of the K-Y Track Club, pushed me to do things that I didn't know I could do on the track and taught me how to dig deeper into myself and find the things that were there without me even knowing. I also learned about being mentally tough and fighting through superficial physical pain. Learning how to break through that simple mind-over-matter ideal was invaluable in my pursuit of higher successes as an athlete and in life in general.

Watching US Congressman Cleo Fields come of age politically was huge for raising my belief in what I could accomplish in my life. Cleo was my original Barack Obama before I—or virtually anyone else on a national scene, for that matter—had heard of Obama. Cleo came from extremely modest circumstances and went on to become the youngest-ever elected official to statewide office in Louisiana and then national office. Because of the early relationship that he built with my father, starting when he was only fifteen, I got an inside look at the highest levels of national politics. It's not that I understood at that age, but to be able to meet with and converse with the likes of the vice president, Al Gore, on two different occasions and to be the emcee of a youth program featuring the Speaker of the House, Tom Foley, were big deals. Both of those opportunities were afforded to me based on my relationship with Cleo. He was young, but based on what I saw him do, I believed that I could do great and extremely significant things beyond the basketball court. I remember being so proud when I would see Cleo interacting with the president and national heads of state. I knew his story and knew that people had laughed at him when he was asked in middle school what he wanted to be when he grew up. He said, while having patched-up pants and shoes with holes in them, "The president of the United States!" He still believed, and based on a dogged persistence, tremendous belief, and extreme faith, he made it happen. He would let me tag along, listen in, and absorb things every once in a while. I will always be grateful for the time that he spent with me, and even today we talk, and every now and then he'll offer advice on different things and allow me to aid him in areas that I have expertise in.

The next person who was a mentor outside of my parents and a few of my teachers was a close friend of my dad's, Ben Jeffers. Jeffers served as secretary of state for Louisiana's governor, Edwin Edwards, in the late 1970s and into the 1980s. He was the first black statewide elected official and was definitely one of the nation's best political strategists and behind-the-scenes movers and shakers. Ben and his wife, Salomi, attended church with our family, and I always loved going over to their home and spending time just talking to him about politics and life. To me, Ben and Salomi's home was like a museum. They had beautiful works of art from African American artists and a great library. He had such a wealth of factually established consciousness in many areas, especially politics, and his way of sitting down, talking to me, and explaining things made it even that much better. He was also a great dresser, and during my later years in high school and into college, as I started to grow, he would pass clothes on to me. NICE CLOTHES. I owned and wore my first designer suits—Canali, Hugo Boss, and Armani—thanks to Ben Jeffers. Ben's calm but extremely assured and confident nature and his substantial wealth of knowledge in politics were, along with my father and Cleo Fields, a major reason why I ran for student council and always considered the possibility of running for office. I learned from both Cleo Fields and Ben Jeffers that a difference could be made from "inside of the system," and that it was a realistic possibility for me to be involved in that process. With those two as early mentors in my life, it's a wonder that I wasn't dragged in the direction of politics right after deciding to hang up my tennis shoes.

The last mentor I'll cover—but certainly not the last person to make a significant impact on me—was the man who became a mentor of mine once I decided to walk away from basketball. Bill Whittle had played ball with my father at LSU during the early 1970s and had started and finished school a year ahead of him. I originally thought that we would grow a thriving but specifically business relationship. What has grown has become much more than just a business-based relationship. I've learned a great deal from him about building and maintaining personal relationships and a host of other invaluable things.

After leaving LSU, having had a nice college career, and unsuccessfully trying out with the then New Orleans Jazz, Mr. Whittle took a job as the first head basketball coach and taught social studies at the largest public high school in Baton Rouge at the time, Tara High School. Mr. Whittle was only twenty-two years old when he took the job. Whittle coached and taught for eight years before a company called A. L. Williams found him and, along with developing his immense work ethic, changed his life forever. Within four years, Coach Whittle went from earning $16,500 during his last year of coaching basketball, track, and football and teaching history to having $1 million in cash saved and earning nearly $700,000 a year. Over his career, Whittle has established himself as a major and preeminent player with the company that is easily one of the greatest business stories in American business. When he found me at the end of 2003, he was already well established, earning over $200,000 monthly and, for the most part, doing it passively by conducting meetings with his organization all over the southeastern and northeastern parts of the country. When I thought about being in business, doing it the way that Bill Whittle was doing it was extremely attractive, and the more I spent time around him, the more attractive it became. In addition to the major things like truly being able to make a REAL hands-on difference and impact in people's lives with what my business could offer and making a relatively significant amount of money without a great deal of risk, I realized I could experience an interesting CONTROLLED fame within the Primerica network. Whittle's way of treating people one on one, coaching them, and leading them in general and his ability to speak in front of a crowd were all things that I marveled at and took a great deal from. Watching how Bill Whittle conducted his entire life was a learning experience. Although we differed in some of our beliefs about politics, everything else about our thought processes was identical, and it was the first time that it became abundantly clear to me that, from a mentorship perspective, you don't have to be 100 percent in alignment with a person to be able to glean a great deal of knowledge from that person. Coach Bill Whittle and I have built an amazing association that has far exceeded our business relationship. I've learned a great deal from him, and his thought process has greatly influenced how I approach my business and life. I was extremely blessed to be raised by two amazing parents who set me on a path to success, thanks to the way they got me thinking, and being able to have another example of extreme success in business and in interpersonal interactions with Bill Whittle has been an added bonus.

Another interesting take on mentorship that I believe I would be totally remiss in not mentioning is the impact that President Barack Obama has had on taking certain limitations away from my thinking and taking away all excuses for not being as successful as possible. Now, before you anti-Obama fans close the book, I want you to read intently. Since the United States was formed, no person other than a WHITE MAN had been president of this great country. My ancestors had been brought in the bowels of slave ships to the United States from western African countries to be sold as property. Having been raised by extremely proud, ethnically conscious, intelligent, and entrepreneurially successful parents, I had always been told that I could do or be anything I wanted in life, but the reality in my mind always seemed to be that I could be anything I wanted in life, EXCEPT for that. It went without being said, but it was understood that that saying applied to everything outside of being president of the United States of America. Do I totally and wholeheartedly believe in ALL of President Obama's policies? No, but I would most definitely vote for him again if I could. When Barack Obama was elected president of the most powerful nation in the world, all limits and excuses were removed. I teared up that night because I could truly believe that anything was possible if I did the work, stayed true to who I was, and prayed and believed I could make it happen. President Obama has served two terms without any scandal or misstep, despite several opportunities where his resolve has been tested personally and politically. This illustrates in my mind how amazing he truly is as a husband, father, leader, and as a man. He has definitely served as a mentor, albeit from afar.

It's very rare that someone hits the lottery once, much less multiple times. But with my mentors and the people I was blessed to be surrounded with, as well as the ones I was able to surround myself with directly and indirectly in my life, I would compare it to the equivalent of winning several lotteries! There are mentors who are in your life for a season, and sometimes you have mentors who remain with you throughout your whole life. I've been able to experience both and am extremely grateful; I understand why, in almost all cases of success, MENTORSHIP of some type plays an integral role. I hope that I'm able to make an impact on people the way that so many people have made such an amazing difference in my own life.

Because of the business in which I operate, mentorship is everything. I often say to people, "I exist in your life for one primary reason, and that's to help you achieve the success in this business and in your life that you desire." I honestly cannot think of anything more rewarding than aiding people in defining and accomplishing their goals. That's what mentorship is all about, and I truly consider it a privilege to help people achieve levels of success beyond what they may have seen as possible for them prior to coming in contact with me—directly or indirectly.

Think about the game "follow the leader." The person who doesn't do exactly as the leader does loses the game. I've often seen that when it comes to mentorship and coachability. There are many people who profess to want to take their lives in specific areas to higher heights, yet they choose to be selectively coachable, or partially mentored, based on their level of comfort or convenience. In terms of mentorship, it became abundantly clear to me early on that comfort and convenience were not areas I needed to be focused on. To win at "follow the leader," EXACT mirroring of the leader is necessary. Successes in business, or many other things, for that matter, are not a lot different at all.

Mentorship allows you to expose yourself to greatness. Whether it is through an audio book or a seminar, or if you're blessed as I've been to deal with your mentors in person, the primary benefit is exposure! In many cases a mentor will help you see things and experience things in ways that you never would have processed had you not had the opportunity to receive the valuable coaching.

WSTM LESSONS LEARNED

1. Who is serving as your mentor? If you don't currently have a mentor, get one quickly. Remember that you may have multiple mentors based on the different areas of your life. You should obtain mentors in the areas of your life that matter the most to you.

2. Who are you mentoring right now? In what area(s) of your life are you experiencing a level of success that others may aspire to achieve?

3. Truly value any type of relationships with those who've achieved success doing what you're striving to achieve. Never take for granted opportunities to be mentored or waste the time of someone willing to mentor you by not implementing the mentor's coaching tips.

4. What books are you reading or audio books are you listening to that are serving as mentorship opportunities for you right now?

Chapter 18

WINNING IN BUSINESS AND
HELPING OTHERS ACHIEVE

*To truly motivate others 1) discover what
their motives, desires and drivers are
2) genuinely connect with and support them
from the heart. —Rasheed Ogunlaru*

*Every individual must be given the opportunity
to unearth his/her highest potential.
—Lailah Gifty Akita*

I cannot say that I did not have a real belief that I would be able to be successful as a businessman. Everything I had set out to do in my life, other than having a successful and long-term NBA career, I had been able to accomplish based on work ethic, an ability to focus, and sheer will. I also had a great example in my parents of what success in business looked like. If I was going to be coached one on one by someone who was already extremely successful and who would benefit from me being successful, I figured that it was only a matter of time before I would be able to start experiencing success in business myself. From the concept

I originally learned from my mom and my subsequent adoption of the mentality that "how you do ANYTHING is how you do EVERYTHING," a huge difference was made. That thought helped me to understand that not only could I be successful outside of being a student athlete, but I could excel to any level if I was willing to do what it took to achieve success.

I did discover, especially in the type of business in which I chose to make a difference and make a living, that relationships are EVERYTHING. That was definitely something that I had to grow to understand and value more. My leadership style early on during my life was to get in the gym, outwork everyone, and make sure however I could that my teammates knew that I outworked them. I wanted them to recognize that at the end of the game, I had earned the right to take the shot, have the ball, or whatever. I understood the value of relationships to a certain extent, but I had a "lone ranger" mentality about leadership. I was the guy who would put in a lot of extra time, but as an athlete, I really don't remember consistently getting any other guys to step up their levels of commitment beyond just playing harder in practice and games. Looking at Michael Jordan prior to his string of six NBA Championships, he was a one-man crew. When he decided he was truly ready to go to the next level, he enlisted the help of Tim Grover as a personal trainer, and not only did he do extra working out, but inspired other Bulls to come along and improve themselves as well. The decision benefited everyone involved and resulted in the greatest player of all time also becoming one of the greatest winners of all time. From a leadership perspective in business, that's exactly what I realized that I needed to do. I discovered that although my commitment to excellence and being great was a definite requirement for my successes, if I wanted to achieve the next level of greatness, it would require me to get others to truly believe that they could achieve levels beyond what they may have believed were possible for them prior to coming in contact with me. I learned that leadership summed up in one word is INFLUENCE! Influence meant I could get others to do things that they probably wouldn't have believed they could do without me. The next level of influence would be to get them to buy into the process, take ownership of it, and sell other people on why they should get involved too, and so on. I discovered early on in my business career that the same things that were required to achieve success outside of business were also required to achieve success in business, AND THEN SOME!

Obtaining certain skills is of paramount importance in reaching certain levels of success in business. SALES SKILLS, PEOPLE SKILLS, and LEADERSHIP SKILLS are all crucial skills to attain. It's funny when I hear people talk about not being a salesperson, or stating, "I'm just not a people person." Those statements are a big reason why people remain in the situation that they're in. The reality is that we are all constantly selling someone on something. As children we are selling our parents on why we have to have that specific snack, game, pair of shoes, or phone. As we grow up, we are selling prospective dates on why they would benefit from letting us take them out, or selling the teacher on why we deserve an opportunity to make that assignment up, or we might negotiate with our parents to extend our curfews. Then as adults, we make the ultimate sale of convincing someone to spend the rest of his or her life with us. For many, that is a LONG sales process with several counteroffers and probably times when both parties consider walking away from the deal. Think about it—from the moment we start dating someone whom we see any real potential in, the sales process begins. In fact, just to get the whole process kicked off took SALES SKILLS and PEOPLE SKILLS.

You may dismiss these examples as simply life experiences, but I discovered that the true difference between ultra-successful people and normal people is their ability to transfer these same skills we all have in certain areas to every area of their lives. The ability of ultra-successful people to transfer these skills enhances not only their lives in general but also serves as a way for them to improve on their already strong skill sets.

Ownership meant a great deal to me, and due to my being raised and taught, by two extremely entrepreneurial people, my parents, I truly valued the idea of owning a business. When I realized that I could OWN my own agency in the most literal sense of the word and assist others in building their own agencies—which would in turn grow my own empire—I was immediately smitten by the ownership opportunity with the company. I think I've also done a good job in explaining my belief surrounding hard work and respecting any process that led to successful results. Even without the knowledge of a formal sales process prior to going into business, I innately understood that some type of sales was a part of every area of life and negotiations.

The concept of a WIN-WIN relationship was always something that I had valued but didn't know truly could exist in the world of business. I loved the idea of being able to mentor others to success and build relationships that were stronger than just a strategic partnership, possibly approaching a family-type relationship. Primerica offered me that opportunity—the opportunity to make a relatively significant amount of money; make a real difference in the lives of clients and business associates; and, for those faithful few willing to truly pay the extremely lucrative price of changing and growing, the opportunity to help them change their financial existence, and in turn their overall existence, forever.

Whether drawing from the lessons I learned in watching my father's masterful interactions with people or my mother's quiet but persistent confidence in her communications with people, I have learned an immense amount. Also, through learning from a master in my chosen profession, Bill Whittle, and gaining access to so many other mentors through books, audio books, and the like, I began learning and growing as a communicator and builder of people. These are the basic concepts taught by Art Williams, the founder of A. L. Williams (the predecessor company for Primerica). Mr. Williams is one of the masters of intercommunication with people, getting the most out of people, and helping people achieve what they, in many cases, didn't know was even possible for themselves. Some of his sage advice urges that "everybody wants to be somebody," "treat people good," and "total commitment is the first step to greatness." I learned from Zig Ziglar that "I can get anything I want in life, as long as I help enough other people get what they want." The basic understanding that, at their core, people want to win, be thought of as someone special, and live a life of significance is the driving factor for me every day as I look to bring value to and impact people in ways that will leave a lasting impression on their lives and on the lives of those around them.

I'm extremely fortunate to have found a company where the focus is on people and truly enhancing the lives of people in a way that is immeasurable. Based on the structure of my business and the opportunities that exist in that structure to assist others in achieving their wildest dreams— and in many cases things they never even dreamed—I've had the chance to have a front-row and first-class seat in watching the growth process of several people who have made significant changes to achieve pretty extraordinary things. There have been some who came into business with me and did not need to make as many changes as others, but it's all been amazing to watch, nonetheless. From highly successful people to twenty-year-old college dropouts, I've witnessed a great deal and played a part in assisting people in the goal-attainment journey of success. I can honestly say that I've cried when seeing others succeed with some guidance from me more than I cried in achieving many of the things that I set out to achieve. I cannot think of anything more fulfilling than helping people achieve something that they may not have achieved had I not pointed them in a certain direction, given them some encouragement during a difficult or dark time, or just told them, "I believe in you!" and sincerely meant it with everything in me to the point where they knew it, and it was fuel to spur them on. I know that talking like this may seem kind of lame or corny to some people, but the reality is that it means EVERYTHING, and IT'S OUR LIVES and THE LIVES OF OTHERS that we're talking about impacting and making a lasting and real difference in.

In relationship to helping others achieve, I've had the humbling experience of seeing the ripple effect of decisions I've made to fight through challenging circumstances to achieve the things I've wanted in life. The ripple effect is the effect that my success has had on those whom, while I was overcoming obstacles, I never knew, and didn't know I would ever meet. It's similar to the domino theory in that had one thing not occurred, so many other things would not have happened, and in turn, so many other people would not have been positively impacted. It's a very powerful and sobering thought that becomes more and more evident the longer that I'm in business. Because of my choice to remain engaged and persistent, there are people in business pursuing their goals and dreams who may not have had an opportunity had I not done what was necessary to succeed. It became clear to me early on that no one would want to hear my story if I wasn't experiencing success, and if I wanted to tell my story the only way was to win! I developed the mentality that me winning was directly related to me helping other people achieve their goals. It was my belief that there was a symbiotic relationship, in which one could not exist without the other. In actuality, that is truly the case in the business that I'm in, but even if a person is not in a business, the success of those around you is still a determining factor in some shape or form of your own success.

I'm extremely fortunate to be able to wake up every morning excited about the day and knowing that I'm in control of my own life and may possibly meet the person today whose life I could change forever. That's a great feeling. It also speaks to the question that many ask often—"When is enough, enough?" I don't know the answer to that question because I haven't gotten there yet. I think about how someone who many would have perceived as having *enough*, Bill Whittle, afforded me the opportunity to accomplish great things and have an ever-reaching impact with an amazing company. Had Bill Whittle decided that he had gotten his and was done, he would have never worked with me. I truly think about that and say that it would be selfish for me to get mine and be gone. Whom would I miss out on having the opportunity to pour into and, in turn, grow more from myself?

WSTM LESSONS LEARNED

1. The number of times that you hit the snooze button on the alarm clock in the morning may be in direct correlation to how excited you are about your life and work experience. Consider this reality and make the necessary changes to improve your excitement and energy surrounding what you do for a living.

2. Are you developing your sales, people, and leadership skills? Regardless of what you do, you will encounter some area of life where it will be necessary that you've sharpened these skills.

3. Being a lone ranger wasn't what I needed to do if I truly wanted to accomplish my goals and dreams. People are more interested in themselves and their goals rather than mine, so I needed to focus on helping them reach their goals, and my accomplishments would naturally follow.

4. Ask yourself, "What's the ripple effect of the decisions I'm making right now?" If the honest answer isn't one you're excited about, CHANGE!

Chapter 19

MEETING AND BUILDING A RELATIONSHIP WITH MY WIFE

Love recognizes no barriers. It jumps hurdles,
leaps fences, penetrates walls to arrive at
it's destination full of hope. —Maya Angelou

You know you're in love when you can't fall
asleep because reality is finally better
than your dreams. —Dr. Seuss

Sometimes when two people pool their talents
and work together toward a joint goal,
they accomplish extraordinary things.
—Angela and Art Williams

Being only a few years and three children into my marriage journey with my amazing wife doesn't nearly qualify me to talk with any extreme certainty like I know exactly what's going on in anyone else's marriage, and that's not what this is about anyway. I have the phenomenal opportunity to learn and grow every day to be a better husband, partner, supporter, friend, lover, cheerleader, coach, mentor, and mentee with and for my wife. I am not delusional enough to attempt to give you advice about relationships or marriage, but I can tell you how my relationship has grown with my compassionate, loving, extremely intelligent, emotionally insightful, sexy, and beautiful wife, Britney Monet Temple, who also happens to be an entrepreneurial and marketing genius. (Did I get all that right, Britney?)

"Are you married?"

That was the line. Those were the words that started it all! After she looked at me, startled and surprised that I had asked her that, and said "No," I proceeded to ask a series of other questions.

"You aren't engaged? You are in a serious relationship, aren't you? Are you waiting to get into this party?" The answers to the second two questions were the same as the first one, and she answered as shocked that I was even asking as she had for the first question. The answer to the last one was, "Yes, but I'm waiting on my friend," to which I replied, "Come on in with me; you don't need to wait in line." I pulled a "G" move as soon as we got into the party at the Lyceum Dean on Third Street in downtown Baton Rouge on that Saturday night, December 22, 2007, by escorting Ms. Britney Monet Hurst into the party and then leaving her to wait on her friend, Avery, while I went and enjoyed the company of several of my boys who had urged me to come out with them and enjoy myself. THANK GOD I heeded the prodding of my friends to come out that night, as I normally didn't. I guess you could tell by the lines I used that I didn't have much "game." I just shot from the hip. Hey, it worked, didn't it? We reconnected that night a couple of hours later and talked in a corner until the party was over, realizing how much we had in common, including many of our friends, and wondering how we had both grown up in the relatively small city of Baton Rouge with many of our friends and family knowing one another, both being heavily involved in sports, and not having any interaction with each other before. That night Britney and I talked until the party was over and left around 1:45 a.m. The next morning, we were both at the same church for the 8:00 a.m. service without even planning it. After the service I invited Britney to a Christmas party that I was having at the house I had just moved into only six months earlier, and she accepted my invitation. That began twenty-one straight days of us seeing each other.

Britney and I had both just come out of serious relationships. I had been engaged to a young lady only seven months earlier before we made a mutual decision to break it off, and she had dated a guy for several years before their relationship had ended. I was enjoying my single life and was not in a hurry to get into a relationship, and although I definitely was looking forward to having and building a family with someone, I had always said that I wasn't going to get married before thirty years old. After having broken off the prior engagement, that seemed like a serious impossibility, and I wasn't the least bit worried about it. My business was growing, and I was enjoying my new home. Britney coming into the picture changed all of that—for the better, I may add—but I can honestly say that I was nervous early on, because things seemed to be going TOO well, and we had so much in common that it was almost scary. At first glance, her independence and entrepreneurial instincts were very attractive to me. She had a modeling agency that she was excited about growing and using to make a real difference in the lives of young ladies, and that was something to be admired in my eyes. Britney had been a SERIOUS athlete, having played professional volleyball overseas after completing her eligibility on a volleyball scholarship at Tulane University in Louisiana. Britney had dominated not only in volleyball in high school, but in track and field and basketball on her way to earning the prestigious honor of 1999 Female High School Athlete of the Year in Louisiana. She also had a magnetism when it came to people that was amazing to me. Her enthusiasm about life in general and about her own life specifically was contagious.

I had learned a great deal from my previous relationship, which was big for me, considering that I was not a serial-relationship person, or someone who always had to be with someone. In fact, my previous relationship had been the first serious relationship I had been involved in that lasted longer than three months. I remember early one morning, after a conversation with a local pastor of a big church that I did not attend, writing down EXACTLY what I wanted in my mate. Britney matched my list verbatim. I really knew after two dates that this was the person I wanted to spend my life with, and that was scary to me so soon after having met her. We were engaged in January of 2009, almost thirteen months after meeting, and were married on August 1, 2009, one month before my thirtieth birthday.

All of this is not to say that everything was perfect. There were some differences. I was definitely an ACTION- and RELATIONSHIP-oriented person, but interestingly enough, I also enjoyed a great deal of STRUCTURE in my life. I took great pride in making my bed up every morning and in putting everything back in "its place" once I finished with it at my house, which, for the most part, meant that other than needing dusting every week, my house stayed pretty straight. STRUCTURE was that LAST thing Britney was focused on! I remember thinking early on, "I'm an 'A' personality type [action-oriented], but Britney is an 'A' on STEROIDS!" She was always on the go, and many times it seemed to me like she was going in circles, but she always had a method to her madness, and although she very rarely took the time to write it down or formally map it out, she always had a plan for what she wanted to accomplish. That was a major difference from me, but I've learned that you don't marry someone to change that person. You marry that person because you love him or her. You love that person as he or she is, and in my case specifically, because of how that person improves you and makes you better. Fortunately for me, my wife is a great example for my daughters to emulate in almost every area. I was taught that the best thing a woman can do for her kids is to be the best woman she can be, and the rest will take care of itself. I had a great example in my mother of a woman who excelled in everything that she made a decision to get involved with and still was there for us.

We have definitely complemented each other extremely well, and especially early on, because she was more in tune to relationships and people's feelings than I was. Along with that female intuition, she helped me a great deal. Looking back, there were probably instances where I should have listened to her more.

In successful partnerships, there's flexibility. There's room for growth and also flexibility and understanding that roles may change and adjust. During my marriage to Britney, she's had to make the majority of the adjustments, and it's been amazing for me to watch her do it all. Her ability to change roles has been fascinating. When we first were married and she helped if the field in the business, that was one role. She actually has still to this day assisted more clients in one month by herself than 95 percent of the active agents in my business, but when that role shifted she excelled there as well. Once we had our first child, her role as a mother kicked into high gear, and although she still stayed engaged with the business, she almost seamlessly made the transition to excel in that role. As our family has grown, Britney's always remained active in our business as well as the other businesses and endeavors that she pursues, as well as staying involved in the community from a civic perspective. Her ability to adapt and become proficient at whatever role is necessary at that time has been a saving grace in our life together.

I think of Britney and me as a POWER COUPLE and a DYNAMIC DUO capable of accomplishing anything together. I really believe that the song by Fabolus and Ne-Yo, "You Make Me Better," applies to us. My favorite line in the song is the hook: "I'm a movement by myself, but we're a FORCE when we're together. Baby, I'm good all by myself, but girl, you MAKE ME BETTER." That's Britney and me. We complement each other so well and enhance what we can offer the world based on our relationship. To me, that's the greatest thing about what we're building together. There is not any area where we subtract or take away from each other's strengths. It's not about addition when we're together; it's about the synergy that's created by multiplication and the compound effect. That's what any great partnership should be about, and other than your spiritual relationship, what partnership is greater than that of marriage?

WSTM LESSONS LEARNED

1. If you're interested in finding a partner, have you written down and clearly defined what you want? You do not have to settle.
2. You must work on making your marriage great, like anything else you want to be great at. Nothing gets better with neglect, including your marriage.
3. Respect the adjustments and changes in roles that will take place, and always give your partner the benefit of the doubt.
4. Give of yourself without expecting anything in return. Because of human nature, this one is the toughest, but the most important!

Chapter 20

BECOMING A FATHER

*Fatherhood is a man's main goal and appointed
purpose in life. —Sunday Adelaja*

*Fatherhood is the greatest education a man
can ever receive. —Asa Don Brown*

Having had the opportunity to travel all over North America speaking about business, success, and the necessary thought processes that lead to goal accomplishment, I've always said that I looked forward to becoming a father and having the opportunity to be a parent and impart belief, encouragement, knowledge, wisdom, life lessons, and an immeasurable amount of love to my children. I believe, like many probably do, that I had phenomenal parents who were a big reason for me experiencing the success and inevitably the life that I have, based on the mind-set that they brainwashed into my psyche early on. I was POSITIVELY BRAINWASHED into being a pretty solid young man, and, in my humble opinion, that's the way it should be. There are enough avenues that exist and are pushing agendas that I wouldn't want my daughters and son exposed to, and it's my job as a parent—and even more so a father—to steer them clear of them and protect them from those potentially dangerous situations.

I am blessed to be the father of Monet Juliet Temple, born on October 7, 2010; Eden Amelia Temple, born on February 11, 2013; and Collis Benton Temple IV, born February 27, 2015. All three of my children are blessings that I could not imagine being without. I've really got to be careful to grow the type of relationships with them that I want. Because of my interesting personality and thought processes about work and the position that I should be putting my children in, I've got to make sure that I spend QUALITY time with them. I can honestly say that it has to be an INTENTIONAL thing, because every once in a while, I'll say that I'm spending time with them, but I'm just watching TV while they play and run around me. That's not real QUALITY time. My mentality is to make the time valuable and memorable. In my mind, all the work is more than worth it, so that I truly can experience the type of QUALITY and QUANTITY that I want to with them and my wife. Fortunately, I get to build my businesses to the point of true operation without me HAVING to be engaged, because I want to be able to be as engaged with them as possible. Not that I would EVER truly slow down—I know myself—but I definitely want to be in a position where I could if I wanted to, and I know that I want to be able to coach my daughters and son all the way up in whatever they're involved with. At the same time, with my business, I want to be able to provide them with the FREEDOM that I was blessed to have based on what my parents worked to build.

Britney was extremely excited about the idea of having children. It was something she would get so emotionally wrapped up in the thought of that she would literally be crying at the possibility of us struggling to have children. I never understood early on why she would get so worked up, but I realized that that's how badly she wanted children, and that's how excited she was about being a mother. It is something that I've always admired, and I feel blessed to have a woman who places so much value on her role as a mother.

Teaching and leading my children has been the ultimate learning experience and training ground in leadership. I can imagine how much more I will have the opportunity to learn as they get older, and I'm totally looking forward to it.

I've already begun to learn that many of the same ideals and success principles that led to success in the classroom, on the basketball court, and in the business arena apply in reference to dealing with my children. You've got to put the time in. It has to be a priority, and, when you think about it, what type of true quality of life would I be able to have if I did not have them there to watch them grow and mature as people? Quality of life is about the time we spend with those we love and the money we make to enjoy the time with those people at an even higher level. I would have a great life with just Britney, but she would agree that our children have enhanced our lives beyond measure or anything that words could describe.

It's my belief that what I do at this point in my still-young life is to build what will be a legacy that my children will WANT to take over. I want to build a business, lifestyle, and life that makes such an amazing impact on people and is so fun to live that my children would gladly take the reins and want to take over doing the same thing that we do. And if they don't, that would be okay as well. I want them to be fully clear about living their lives the way they want to with the baseline and foundation that Britney and I are able to give to them. With my oldest daughter, before she turned two years old, I started speaking and having her repeat a series of affirmations about herself back to me every morning. In my, and my wife's, mind, it was all about starting the process of building her SELF-esteem and helping her to start to realize her self-worth and the power that she possesses. I would wake her up in the morning, and the first thing I asked her was, "Monet, what are you?" Before too long, she was replying to me, "I'm a LEADER, a CHAMPION, a PRINCESS, a CHILD OF GOD, and a GENIUS!" Monet came up to me a few months before she turned five years old and said, "Daddy, I think I need to start saying that I'm a WINNER too. What do you think about that?" I was so excited about her coming up with that on her own that I couldn't stand it. I planted a seed, and now it's becoming SELF-ESTEEM and it reflects how she sees herself. That's huge to me! We have already started the process of "positive brainwashing" with our second daughter, Eden, and Collis will follow. Think about the power of imparting and imprinting that belief in their heads since before they were two years old and not just having them repeat it to me like a parrot, but reminding them throughout the day at every opportunity of what a great leader would do in certain situations or how a leader would act based on the circumstances, and how champions react to experiencing things that may not necessarily be exactly what they want. I'm working with my children to teach them the value of those affirmations and strengthen their knowledge of what they are and can become. In my mind, there really is nothing more exciting than watching my children grow into men and women who represent God, themselves, my wife and me, our family, their community, and our country in a way that we can be proud of. I don't believe it's being overly melodramatic. IT'S ONLY OUR CHILDREN, right? It's only the next generation that will carry the torch and either take things to another level or drive them into the dirt. In my estimation, we don't just have an opportunity, but an obligation to do better by our kids and put them in a position to have more, become more, and be better than we are and will be. That's what it's about, right? It's all about advancing your family to the next level in every way possible.

I mentioned earlier that, based on my business, I've been able to experience the unique opportunity to speak to crowds all over North America, both small (ten to twenty) and large (over thirty thousand). The comments and compliments that have made the greatest impact and meant the most to me have revolved around me making a difference in people's lives from a perspective of something I said helping them with their children and parenting. To me, that's what making a true impression is about. That's how I can make a difference that will sustain itself and continue to grow long after I'm gone.

When I think of my role as a parent, it's so significant because a primary reason for me doing what I've been able to do is based on how I was trained, taught, reared, and parented. It's an understatement in my mind to say that being a parent is an honor and privilege. There aren't words to describe how critically important my role as a parent is. All parents have an obligation to do their level best to give their children the tools they need to compete in the world. Whether people are well educated or not so well educated, they can impart love, compassion, confidence, respect, work ethic, and values that make all the difference in their children's lives long after they're out of their parents' care. Because I believe that most people are not hypocrites, I think that when they don't give these things to their children, it is because they may not have them themselves. If we owe it to anyone, we owe it to our kids to constantly become better versions of ourselves, to improve and be examples of what they can be and where they can go.

WSTM LESSONS LEARNED

1. Are you POSITIVELY BRAINWASHING your children? Are you being the gatekeeper of the influences in their lives to the best of your ability? Parenting and raising children is an amazing opportunity to put some phenomenal programming into a person who will one day be an adult and could make an amazing impact on society. Are you treating your opportunity as a parent that way?
2. Are you serving as the best version of yourself for yourself, and therefore for your children?
3. Self-esteem is more important than esteem from others.
4. Do affirmations with your children. It's amazing to see them adopt these things as realities about themselves.
5. Apply leadership principles to your most important duty—as a parent!

Chapter 21

THE FUTURE

*Life gets very exciting when you've got a
plan and realize that today counts
for tomorrow, and that you and God
are in control! —Collis Temple III*

*Am I MAXIMIZING my existence? Do I
truly look forward to every day?
Are the best days of my life still ahead of me?—
YES, YES, and YES! —Collis Temple III*

I look toward my and my family's future with so much excitement and
enthusiasm! Many may look and say that I've already arrived, but in
my mind, there's so much more to do and so many more people to help,
touch, impact, and affect that I'm blessed to be just getting started with
the distinct opportunity to do something very special.

It has always been interesting to me how God always seems to work
things out in the most subtle ways. Sometimes it's BOLDLY obvious; other
times, things happen in a course of action that you don't even realize until
you look back and think, "Wow! Look how that situation worked itself out!"

I think a great example of this came in early 2015 when I was appointed to the Louisiana Board of Regents by the governor. The Board of Regents is the fifteen-person body that makes the decisions about the direction of higher education in the state. When I think back to my grandfather having to deal what he had to deal with in his desire to attend LSU to earn his master's degree and having the state legislature appropriate funds for him to attend Michigan State rather than allowing him to attend LSU, it blows my mind. Think about it; a man wants to attend the flagship school for higher education in the state he lives in and grew up in, but due to the racial climate and the way things simply were at the time, he is not allowed to do so. Despite the setback, this man still had the wherewithal to remain composed, to not be bitter about his present, and to keep a hopeful and active mind on his future vision. Based on that vision, nearly twenty years later, his son is pursued by the same school that turned him down. He even has the governor of the state court him and his son for him to allow his son to break the color lines at the school in a specific area of athletics. Although it's important that the young man can play ball, it can't just be about athletics, because a precedent must be set. The young man attends the university, excels as an athlete and a student, and opens the door for many others to follow under much easier conditions. He goes on to make a great impact in his own right far beyond what he accomplishes on the athletic field of play and has three sons and a daughter. All of his sons go on to play college athletics, and two of them actually follow in their father's footsteps and the shadow of their grandfather's vision and go to their father's alma mater, the flagship university, and earn degrees while competing athletically on scholarship. One of the grandsons goes on to earn not only his undergraduate degree but also his master's degree and even starts working toward his PhD—all paid for by the same university that would not allow his grandfather to attend. The story would almost seem too good to be true at that point, but add to it that the grandson of that man ends up being named to the highest board and decision-making entity in the entire state regarding all of higher education, and you've got something movie worthy. The reality about the Board of Regents appointment is that it's simply another opportunity to serve and make a positive impact on the people in the state of Louisiana. Ironically, you've got to believe it's much more than coincidence that put this course of action in place over sixty years ago. It was the vision of a man who passed away over twenty years before seeing his own namesake be in a position to make a real difference in an arena where he himself was not allowed to even participate.

You may find it interesting that I would start off the chapter titled "The Future" with a story about the past, but that's simply because it's my belief that any success that we're to have in the future will be based on us growing and learning from our past—learning from our successes and our failures, from our ups and our downs. I learned from Bill Whittle that the best way to use the past is like a BOOK to learn from rather than a HAMMER to beat yourself up with.

In using my daily planner, an integral part that enables greater levels of success to occur is the "Autopsy" part of the planner, where I make note of the things I did well that day that led to success and the things that didn't foster the result that I wanted. The successes are noted to make sure that I repeat them, and the unsuccessful things are also noted so they aren't repeated. The reason I know my future will be greater than the past is because I'm learning from my mistakes, and although it's inevitable that I will make mistakes in the future, it won't be the same mistakes over and over again. The reality of knowing that I'm literally getting better every day, based on growing from my successes and mistakes, ensures that my future will be better and brighter. I have positive expectations in terms of my mentality that no matter how challenging or how amazing my current situation is, tomorrow will be better.

When you think back about great leaders and where great revolutions took place, you don't have to look very far. The civil rights movement in the United States during the 1960s is an outstanding example that I personally am not doing enough and, like many others, am capable of doing more and making more of an impact. When I look at those leading that movement and inciting the change that would eventually take place and change a nation, I don't know how people with anything in them can't feel like they should be doing more and making more of a difference. We can ALL get involved, and we can all make some type of difference and impact. Martin Luther King Jr. said, "Anyone can be great, because anyone can serve."

I read a great book that was a simple and quick read years ago called *Go for No*, and from that book, I gained and adopted a life maxim that has sparked a very interesting and introspective way of thinking for me. Contrary to popular belief, the opposite of success is NOT failing. In true objective reality, the opposite of success is SETTLING for where you are and not attempting to grow and become a better version of yourself. When we cease striving to become better versions of ourselves, cease to make our families better, cease to improve in our professions, and cease to make our communities better places to live, what are we really living for? What are we saying about what we should be leaving as a legacy to the next generation that comes after us? I have NEVER heard of, nor have I personally ever experienced, ANY success without dealing with something that seems like failure being a part of the process. Anyone running away from failure or afraid of failure will surely be missing the opportunity to achieve any level of significant success. The reality is, under no circumstances does SUCCESS occur without being intertwined in some way with FAILURE! Be aggressive about going after the success you desire, and don't be shy about dealing with the failures that will inevitably come with that success!

When I talk about working like a slave and thinking like a master, I'm referring to working like a slave tirelessly toward GREATNESS and MASTERY of whatever you endeavor to achieve, and thinking like a master toward an amazing VISION and FUTURE to ultimately accomplish your MISSION. Be a SLAVE to the daily habits and practices that will lead to your success in whatever you endeavor to succeed at. Be a MASTER of your thoughts with the mentality that the future will be amazingly better and will yield success beyond your wildest imagination, because you are going to WILL it and WORK it into existence!

WSTM LESSONS LEARNED

1. Think about a situation that you may be dealing with and not seeing a positive end to. Understand that, many times, the situation will be resolved in a way that you would never have thought possible. Be excited about the future, understanding that when you control what you can, everything else will more than likely work itself out.

2. Ask yourself, "Am I SETTLING, or am I going for it and dealing with the things that SEEM like FAILURES, but at further glance are actually leading toward my success?" Look at your failures in terms of how they're improving you and therefore getting you closer to success.

3. What are the habits you've become a slave to that are aiding you in your success? Determine what you want, then what you need to do to achieve that goal. Last, be honest with yourself about what's holding you back from achieving that goal—remove the obstacle!